KEDLESTON ROAD

Repositioning
Higher Education

SRHE and Open University Press Imprint
General Editor: Heather Eggins

Current titles include:

Mike Abramson *et al.* (eds): *Further and Higher Education Partnerships*
Catherine Bargh, Peter Scott and David Smith: *Governing Universities*
Ronald Barnett: *Improving Higher Education*
Ronald Barnett: *Limits of Competence*
Ronald Barnett: *The Idea of Higher Education*
Tony Becher (ed.): *Governments and Professional Education*
Hazel Bines and David Watson: *Developing Professional Education*
John Bird: *Black Students and Higher Education*
Jean Bocock and David Watson (eds): *Managing the Curriculum*
David Boud *et al.* (eds): *Using Experience for Learning*
Ann Brooks: *Academic Women*
Angela Brew (ed.): *Directions in Staff Development*
Frank Coffield and Bill Williamson (eds): *Repositioning Higher Education*
Rob Cuthbert: *Working in Higher Education*
Roger Ellis (ed.): *Quality Assurance for University Teaching*
Maureen Farish *et al.*: *Equal Opportunities in Colleges and Universities*
Shirley Fisher: *Stress in Academic Life*
Sinclair Goodlad: *The Quest for Quality*
Diana Green (ed.): *What is Quality in Higher Education?*
Susanne Haselgrove (ed.): *The Student Experience*
Robin Middlehurst: *Leading Academics*
Henry Miller: *The Management of Change in Universities*
Jennifer Nias (ed.): *The Human Nature of Learning: Selections from the Work of M.L.J. Abercrombie*
Keith Noble: *Changing Doctoral Degrees*
Gillian Pascall and Roger Cox: *Women Returning to Higher Education*
Graham Peeke: *Mission and Change*
Moira Peelo: *Helping Students with Study Problems*
John Pratt: *The Polytechnic Experiment*
Tom Schuller (ed.): *The Changing University?*
Peter Scott: *The Meanings of Mass Higher Education*
Michael Shattock: *The UGC and the Management of British Universities*
Harold Silver and Pamela Silver: *Students*
John Smyth (ed.): *Academic Work*
Geoffrey Squires: *First Degree*
Kim Thomas: *Gender and Subject in Higher Education*
David Warner and Elaine Crosthwaite (eds): *Human Resource Management in Higher and Further Education*
David Warner and Charles Leonard: *The Income Generation Handbook*
David Warner and David Palfreyman (eds): *Higher Education Management*
Graham Webb: *Understanding Staff Development*
Sue Wheeler and Jan Birtle: *A Handbook for Personal Tutors*
Thomas G. Whiston and Roger L. Geiger (eds): *Research and Higher Education*
John Wyatt: *Commitment to Higher Education*

Repositioning Higher Education

Edited by
Frank Coffield and
Bill Williamson

Society for Research into Higher Education
& Open University Press

Published by SRHE and
Open University Press
Celtic Court
22 Ballmoor
Buckingham
MK18 1XW

and 1900 Frost Road, Suite 101
Bristol, PA 19007, USA

First published 1997

A catalogue record of this book is available from the British Library

ISBN 0 335 19716 7 (pb)   0 335 19715 9 (hb)

Library of Congress Cataloging-in-Publication Data

Repositioning higher education / edited by Frank Coffield and Bill
  Williamson.
      p. cm.
   Includes bibliographical references and index.
   ISBN 0–335–19715–9 (hardcover). — ISBN 0–335–19716–7 (pbk.)
   1. Education. Higher—Aims and objectives—Great Britain.
 2. Education. Higher—Social aspects—Great Britain. 3. Education.
 Higher—Economic aspects—Great Britain. 4. Education. Higher—
 Great Britain—Administration. I. Coffield, Frank.
 II. Williamson, Bill. 1944– .
 LA637.R46 1997
 378.41—dc21   96–47781
                                                              CIP

Typeset by Graphicraft Typesetters Limited, Hong Kong
Printed in Great Britain by St Edmundsbury Press Ltd, Bury St Edmunds, Suffolk

Contents

List of Contributors

Ronald Barnett is currently Professor of Higher Education and Dean of Advanced Courses at the Institute of Education, University of London. Previously, he was employed by the Polytechnic of London, and at the Council for National Academic Awards, before joining the Institute of Education in 1990. His most recent publications include *The Limits of Competence* (1994), *Improving Higher Education: Total Quality Care* (1992) and *The Idea of Higher Education* (1990). He is also a former editor of Studies in Higher Education and is a council member of the Society for Research into Higher Education.

Frank Coffield has been Professor of Education in the Department of Education at the University of Newcastle since 1996, having previously worked at the Universities of Durham and Keele. His major publications are on such topics as: juvenile delinquency, the 'cycle of deprivation', youth unemployment, youth and the enterprise culture, vandalism and graffiti, training credits, Training and Enterprise Councils, and drugs and young people. In 1995 he edited a collection of essays entitled *Higher Education in a Learning Society* for DfEE, ESRC and HEFCE. He is currently director of the ESRC £2 million research programme into 'the learning society' from 1994 to 1999.

Chris Duke read history at Cambridge, then qualified as a teacher before lecturing at Woolwich Polytechnic for five years and taking a doctorate part-time at London. From 1966 he lectured in sociology in the Adult Education Department of the University of Leeds before becoming foundation Director of Continuing Education at the Australian National University. In 1985 he became foundation Professor of Continuing Education and Chair of the new Department of Continuing Education at the University of Warwick, and also Pro Vice Chancellor from 1991 to 1995. In 1996 he was appointed Deputy Vice Chancellor, University of Western Sydney. He edited the *International Journal of University Adult Education* from 1971 to 1996, and among his publications is *The Learning University* (Open University Press 1992).

Stephen McNair is Associate Director for Research and Development at the National Institute for Adult Continuing Education, with special responsibility for Higher Education and for Telematics. He is also a Higher Education Adviser to the Department for Education and Employment, working on a range of issues to do with HE and its relevance to the world of work. He has previously worked as a teacher and administrator in all parts of the education system. From 1984 to 1992 he was Head of the National Unit for the Development of Adult Continuing Education. He is an Executive Member of the National Guidance Council, a consultant to the Organisation for Economic Co-operation and Development and a Fellow of the Royal Society of Arts.

Robin Middlehurst is the Director of the Division of Quality Enhancement of the Higher Education Quality Council (HEQC). She has experience of teaching at all levels of education, from primary to adult and joined higher education in 1986. Robin has studied leadership and management and their development in universities at the University of Reading and at the Institute of Education in London. As a result, she wrote *Leading Academics* (1993). Robin joined HEQC in 1993 with a brief to continue her work on leadership and management as they relate to the assurance and enhancement of quality in higher education.

David Robertson is Professor of Public Policy and Education and Director of the Institute for Policy Research at Liverpool John Moores University. He is author of *Choosing to Change – Extending Access, Choice and Mobility in Higher Education* (the Robertson Report 1994). He was responsible for the development and management of the Integrated Credit Scheme, a large credit-based modular scheme at the university. Other recent publications include *Proposals for an Associate Degree – the Search for the 'Missing Link' of British Higher Education* (1994), *Policy Continuity and Progress in the Reform of Post-compulsory Education* (1995) and *Funding the Learning Society* (1995).

Bill Williamson is Professor of Continuing Education, University of Durham. Educated at Regent Street Polytechnic and the University of Durham, his research and publications have been in the fields of the sociology of education, comparative education and social history, and are now centred on the sociology of lifelong learning. He taught sociology at Newcastle Polytechnic and the University of Durham. He has worked in universities in Germany, Turkey and Egypt. He is currently working on projects concerned with the role of higher education in regional, social and economic development.

Preface

These essays are meant to provoke debate. Each was written for a seminar series on higher education and each has been modified in the light of discussions following its formal presentation. We very much hope this will happen to the ideas developed in these essays as they reach a broader audience.

The editors are grateful to the contributors for their positive involvement in the seminars upon which this volume is based. We are grateful, too, to the Vice Chancellor of the University of Durham, Professor Evelyn Ebsworth, and Professor Laing Barden, formerly of the University of Northumbria, for hosting and chairing two of the seminars. The Principal of University College Stockton, Mr John Hayward, also hosted one of the seminars and we record our thanks to him here.

The University of Durham, through the Department of Adult and Continuing Education and the School of Education, provided funds to make the seminar series possible. All those who attended contributed greatly to the success of the series. We hope this volume does justice to their contribution.

1

The Challenges Facing Higher Education

Frank Coffield and Bill Williamson

Somebody told *you* and you hold it as an article of faith, that higher education is an unassailable good. This notion is so dear to you that when I question it you become angry. Good. Good, I say. Are not those the very things which we should question? I say college education, since the war, has become so a matter of course, and such a fashionable necessity, for those either of or aspiring *to* the new vast middle class, that we *espouse it*, as a matter of right, and have ceased to ask, 'What is it good for?'

(Mamet 1993)

Industrialization of the language of education

One of the many aspects of higher education which this book questions is the recent industrialization of the language used in the debate. For example, students have become 'customers' or 'consumers' as well as 'inputs and outputs', heads of department are openly described as 'line managers' and many vice chancellors now prefer to be called 'chief executives'. The length of a degree course has been changed to 'the product's life cycle', lecturers no longer teach but 'deliver the curriculum' and aims and objectives have been replaced by 'learner outcomes' and by ubiquitous, vacuous and interchangeable 'mission statements'. Financial cuts are now presented as 'efficiency gains', short, cheap courses are claimed to be 'cost-effective' and staff are no longer made redundant, but institutions 'restructure', 'downsize' or 'rightsize'. Who can object if their institution decides to reach its right or optimal size? Understanding is being replaced by 'competence', knowledge by 'information', and education itself is being transformed into a mass commodity to be bought and sold in the market place. Most revealing of all, possible scenarios for the future of this country are called 'visions for UK plc' – the industrial model has reached its zenith, but the horizons and aspirations on offer are those of the public limited company.

This book presents seven alternative and more ambitious visions of what higher education could become in this country; a starting point is the rejection of the industrialization of the language and the downgrading of certain key values within education by the new vocabulary. This is not a pedantic or a typically 'academic' concern for words and their 'correct' usage; there are more serious issues at stake. For instance, the language we use encapsulates our values, it conditions our thinking and so predisposes us to act differently. Euphemisms such as 'efficiency gains' are being used in an attempt to disguise the severity of the cuts being imposed on the system. The new vocabulary, which even ten years ago was derided and resisted in senior common rooms up and down the country, is slowly becoming the common and taken-for-granted parlance of academic managers. A new mindset is being created, a new agenda is being formed and a new curriculum is being constructed.[1] In this way the critics of the education service have limited and re-ordered the terms of the debate to their advantage; the very nature of education has been misrepresented by this transplanted vocabulary and the contribution education can and should make to the common good is being ignored. The whole of education is being translated into the language of industry and is being reinterpreted as a purely economic domain in need of industrialization (see Poerksen 1995: 53).

Ronald Barnett argues in the following chapter that the new language also reflects the changing relationships between higher education, knowledge and society and, more specifically, the new language heralds the introduction of more industrialized forms of teaching and learning, as predicted by Otto Peters (Keegan 1994). Shortly before his death Dennis Potter claimed that the trouble with words is that you never know whose mouth they have been in last, but in this case the source of the infection is not in dispute.

The main purpose of this introductory chapter is to review briefly the main challenges which currently face higher education and to argue that we need a new model, or preferably a set of competing models, to stimulate a public debate about the future of higher education. The five contributors (who each spoke in a series of seminars on 'the future of higher education' organized by the editors of this volume and given at the Universities of Durham and Northumberland and at the University College of Stockton in 1995) present their differing visions for higher education in the subsequent chapters. The final chapter lays down the ground rules for the coming debate and establishes a new position for universities in relation to all the major players: government, employers and the professions, university staff and students, and the general public. The introductory and concluding chapters were first written by Frank Coffield and Bill Williamson respectively, but there has since been such sharing of ideas and switching of sections that only joint authorship captures the extent of our collaboration.

The central argument of this book can be put simply: the universities, despite all the changes they have made, have not responded and are not responding, with sufficient speed or at an appropriate level, to the technological, economic, social and demographic changes of the past twenty years; in short, the old elite model has run its course and needs to be replaced.

A second theme which will be developed is that the modern *economic imperative* – that dominant discourse of gaining a competitive edge over 'rivals' who used to be called 'trading partners' – tells only half the story. It needs to be matched by a *democratic imperative*, which argues that a learning society worthy of the name ought to deliver social cohesion and social justice as well as economic prosperity to *all* its citizens. It will be claimed that market forces are polarizing British society and that there are structural features of the labour market in the UK which militate against the growth of the type of education and training culture needed if Britain is to become a learning society. David Raffe (1992) has, for example, argued that, instead of constantly reforming education to solve the problems of the labour market, it is now necessary to reform the labour market to solve some educational problems.

Before we turn to such arguments, it is worth observing that the new language of education exhibits some, but not all, of the characteristics of 'plastic words', as described by Uwe Poerksen (1995: 22): the new reality dispenses with the question of value, it is impoverished in content, it contains the appearance of an insight, it paints over controversy and it is historically disembedded. To prevent ourselves falling into the same trap, the changes still required of higher education will now be placed in an historical context.

Higher education in the twentieth century

Eric Hobsbawm (1994) has characterized the twentieth century as the age of extremes. Unable to say what the future holds, though hopeful that it might yet be better than the past, Hobsbawm is at least clear on two things. First, with the collapse of communism an era of history has ended. Second, although no one can know how history will unfold, the past is no longer a guide to the future.

Hobsbawm has in mind a vast canvas of ideas and of changes which have transformed human societies in the twentieth century. The focus here on higher education is much more limited but the necessity of retaining a wide historical perspective on what forces are acting to shape its future is compelling. For the same can be said of higher education as can be said for the century as a whole: an era has ended and what has gone before no longer provides a credible model for the future.

But the parallel can be pushed too far. The moments of change which even now are defining the social and political contours of the Third Millennium are beyond both our detailed understanding and control. They are global in reach, cumulative and in their impact both unintended and unpredictable. Despite our massive ability to plan and control what we do, the only certainty in 'risk societies' like our own is uncertainty (Beck 1992). In the world of higher education, however, we are in principle at least, but within limits, well placed to define the futures we want and to exercise influence to achieve them.

The ability of those who work in universities to do this reflects their professional commitment to understand the world in a detailed and critical way and to engage confidently in public debates about policy in higher education. The voice of universities in these matters may not be the most powerful one in the debate. It is, however, an important one. The experience of British universities in the past two decades has been one of domination from the outside. Universities have changed in profound ways over this period: student numbers have increased, curricula have been redesigned and management structures have been fundamentally revamped. But as Peter Scott (1995) and David Robertson (this volume) have both noted, the impetus for change has come from without. People who work in higher education now have a unique opportunity to help to define the direction of change from within.

They can do so in the knowledge that the shape of higher education in the advanced industrial societies in the twenty-first century has not been predetermined. It could yet be more open and flexible than recent trends might suggest. Higher education institutions could have much more public support than they currently enjoy. Universities could and should be much more decisively engaged in meeting the lifelong training and education needs of people in employment. Higher education institutions should be the leaders in defining the use of the new information technology in the development of innovative forms of teaching and learning.

Universities are now only one of the key players in generating new knowledge through research, and they no longer have an exclusive role in the further development of highly qualified professionals. Nevertheless, they still have a vital role in basic research, in evaluating public policies and in forming multidisciplinary teams to tackle a range of major problems facing modern societies.

These cover questions about the environment, and the consequences of technological and demographic change, including migration, on the social structures of modern societies and much else besides. Matthias Finger (1995) has argued persuasively that the solution to all of these complex problems requires new learning, new ideas and new ways of thinking. Universities, he argues, must help people and organizations in modern societies to 'learn their way out' of the problems they face. They must position themselves to do so and be engaged directly and creatively with the problems of the society which sustains them.

Being in the business of discovering and disseminating knowledge and of recreating new generations of professionals, universities are among the most important institutions of the knowledge-based information economy. As bodies uniquely specialized to test out all claims to knowledge, they have a role to play in public life, in helping people to understand their world in a critical way and in promoting active debate about democratic values and morality. To do so, however, they themselves will have to change.

In the concluding chapter we sketch out some of the ways in which higher education must change to overcome the threats it faces and to define new roles for itself in the new century. The core of the argument is this: universities must themselves change, as otherwise their future will be defined for them by political or business elites. The limits to what they can achieve are, however, set by the societies in which they function. For this reason, it is not sufficient for higher education institutions, universities in particular, to reform themselves. They must seek also to engage in a wide-ranging and critical dialogue within society to secure the conditions of the future growth and sustainable development of both.

A viable model for higher education is inseparable from one for society as a whole. Academics have no right to impose a particular model, but they do have a responsibility to ensure that debates about it are informed, critical and open. They have a responsibility to develop different visions of their own future which can be evaluated in public debate so that public choices in this major area of policy are well informed. It has been one of the weaknesses of higher education, at least in Britain, as the chapter by Robertson in this volume makes clear, that they have not performed this role very well.

In the 'age of extremes' in Europe, universities were at the centre of both the civilization and the conflicts of the century. The scholarly work which took place within them led to some of the most important scientific and technological achievements of the modern world. Universities at their best have been the symbols of hope for a better future for mankind, promoting the values of critical and independent thought, objectivity, truth and intellectual integrity and placing these at the centre of the idea of a higher education.

At their worst, they have been agents of oppressive states. The *gleichgeschaltete Universitäten* of the Third Reich lost all their intellectual independence and, indeed, gave it up all too willingly; as early as 1931 the Nazi Party, for instance, 'enjoyed almost twice as much support in the universities as in the country as a whole' (Joachim Fest 1979: 381). And as Dietrich Bracher (1970: 210) has suggested, the social exclusiveness of the German university in the inter-war years served to nurture and protect reactionary organizations within them. The state-run university institutions of the people's democracies of Eastern Europe, especially those of the German Democratic Republic, offered little resistance to the ideological claims of the state. Academics were all too willing to cash in their objectivity for the benefits of party membership. The intellectual vitality of Eastern Europe was not something nurtured in universities but among intellectual dissidents seeking to live, as Vaclav Havel (1987) has put it, 'within truth'.

Of the many extremes of the twentieth century, arguably the most pernicious and in some ways most fundamental, since is catalysed the ideological politics of the period, has been that of class inequality. Universities have played a role in both reproducing and changing structures of social inequality. They have simultaneously nurtured social, cultural and political elites and opened up opportunities for meritocratic social mobility.

Throughout the post-war period in Europe there has been a remarkable growth in the numbers of students in universities. Between 1960 and 1980, with variations among different European states, the numbers tripled or quadrupled (Laquer 1982). In the United Kingdom there was a fourfold increase in the age participation rate at 18 years, from 8 per cent in 1964 to 33 per cent in 1992. In Britain the most recent expansion in higher education has been even more dramatic. Between 1988/9 and 1993/4, the total number of home students increased by 66 per cent for full-time courses and 33 per cent for part-time courses (CVCP 1995). It was an expansion forced through, with an estimated 30 per cent reduction of the unit of resource per student and severe cuts in capital spending for higher education.

This expansion of student numbers took place within an older model of what a university was and in institutions which had traditionally been socially exclusive. The mass universities of the 1960s and 1970s, some with student numbers in excess of 100,000, such as the Sorbonne or Rome, catered for the needs of the many with courses, teaching and learning styles, curricula and facilities designed for the few.

The rate of growth in student numbers in Britain was slower than in several continental European countries and British higher education institutions remained until the 1990s much smaller than their counterparts elsewhere. The forces driving the expansion were, however, similar: demographic change, rising aspirations and demands from government and industry for better qualified human capital better suited to the needs of industry and a burgeoning service sector.

A general point remains true, however: higher education expanded without fundamental alteration in the elitist model of what constituted a higher education and without altering significantly social class gradients of educational opportunity.

Universities carry the history of this social exclusivity like a dead weight and a constant reproach. It defines the central policy dilemma they have struggled with: the need to expand student numbers without loss to the quality of their teaching and research. And it has limited their capacity to adapt their curricula and their research to respond to new kinds of students and to government pressures to widen their role in relation to both public services and private industry.

The prevailing, though profoundly challenged, model of what a higher education is or should be, which shapes the thinking about higher education both in government and among academics themselves, still recalls the older institutions of the past. Noel Annan, one of the architects of Britain's post-war system of higher education, has characterized the years between 1900 and 1940 as the 'golden age of the Oxbridge undergraduate' and those between 1954 and 1975 as those of the don (Annan 1990: 509). For the former, the university years were 'years of laughter and the love of friends'. For the dons, the post-war years were a time when they could attend to their research, select their students and transmit the high culture of which they were the guardians.

The scaffolds which supported them were those of autonomous, often collegiate, institutions whose freedom to teach and research was either unquestioned, as in Britain, or constitutionally guaranteed, as in the Federal Republic of Germany. Selective in their intake of students, dominated, as Tony Becher (1989) has shown, by the logic of academic subjects, didactic teaching and independently developed research agendas, universities remained for much of the post-war period somewhat aloof from the societies which supported them.

Students within such institutions were typically young, enrolled on full-time courses and, for much of the twentieth century, predominantly male and middle class. Their social and cultural ambience was monastic; even the great Victorian civic institutions ran to an ecclesiastical calendar and their central rituals (gowns, Latin mottoes etc.) harked back to the medieval university.

The problem, of course, as Annan (1990) has explained, and as European governments now acknowledge, is that a system of higher education based on such a model could not be sustainably expanded. His words, reflecting British experiences, are telling:

> It had been right to expand higher education. What had been wrong was to imagine that all students could be given a Rolls-Royce higher education. No country could afford it ... No country could afford centres of excellence (the equivalent of Harvard and Berkeley, the Grandes Ecoles and Max Planck Institutes) and declare that all other universities were to be given equal status.
>
> (Annan 1990: 515–16)

There was always a fiscal constraint on the expansion of higher education. But there were others, just as important. In the 1960s, students objected to the ways in which universities were structured and managed and, during the 1970s and 1980s, governments throughout the whole of the industrialized world began to question the cost and the value of higher education.

They explored ways to transform the model of the university into something much more responsive to the needs of broader constituencies of citizens and criticized universities for their social exclusivity. Decisively, they urged higher education to attend much more closely to the unexplained needs of the economy for skilled manpower and applied research. This was the context for the emergence in the Federal Republic of Germany of the *Gesamthochschulen*, in France of short-cycle higher education and in Britain of the polytechnics.

The detailed story of these changes is well known. Behind the political manoeuvring in higher education policy, however, are the long-term socio-economic and political trends of the twentieth century. The expansion of higher education is a facet of the steady march of democracy, of rising aspirations and of the steadily enlarging view of who is able to benefit from a university education.

Future models of higher education will also be seriously affected by the fiscal crisis of the modern state and the relative decline of the Western industrial economies in the face of global economic competition. And the transformations which have taken place in what universities teach and re-search, in how they themselves are internally managed, are inseparable from the revolutionary changes of the past decades in information techno-logy and in the growth of knowledge.

The age of extremes is coming to an end (though, perhaps, another may be just beginning) but the lid has not been closed on the Pandora's box of evils which shaped it. The political viruses which poisoned higher educa-tion in the twentieth century have not been eradicated. No one seriously imagines that communism or fascism could return in their old guise to place a heavy jackboot of fear on the societies of modern Europe. But national-ism and racism remain potent threats to democratic values and destroy the hopes and aspirations of particular minority communities.

Social hierarchies have flattened, but the gradients of social inequality throughout Europe remain steep and in some countries, notably the United Kingdom, have increased, as the following section will document. Social polarization and social exclusion are taking on new forms, creating cultural fractures of sinister political potential.

The expansion of secondary and higher education throughout the twen-tieth century has not succeeded in building a well educated citizenry cap-able of participating effectively in the political processes which shape their lives. There is a tightening link between knowledge, power and the imper-sonal structures of a global economy. In the information society new frac-ture lines of social inequality are built on differential access to the means of communication, learning and knowledge.

But perhaps more to the point, because millions of people have had no contract with higher education and remain, as the taxpayers who fund it, unconvinced of its merits, they are reluctant to provide the public funds the system itself depends upon. Even in a mass system of higher education where 30–40 per cent of the 18-year-old age group attends, there will still be 60–70 per cent who are asked to pay for the benefits they themselves may never enjoy. Among the older age groups there are much higher proportions of people who never had a chance of higher education. There is an immediate need here for universities to build constituencies of public support in local communities which go much beyond their *alumni*, who have been their prime beneficiaries.

The principal goal of higher education remains the nurturing of a crit-ical understanding among students in whatever discipline they study (Barnett 1993; and in this volume). Throughout Europe, however, governments are keen to strengthen core skills – numeracy, communication, information technology and interpersonal effectiveness – and the vocational relevance of study programmes. They aim to cut the costs of study and to distinguish more clearly among institutions which undertake teaching and research and those which are much more closely tied to technical training (Gellert 1993).

Universities may claim a commitment to the intellect as their primary purpose. Real questions remain, however, about whether such values are realizable in a system structured to nurture narrow competencies in its students and which is attuned more to the needs of the economy – whatever they are in the era of post-Fordist fragmentation – than to any credible version of the democratic intellect in an open society (Barnett 1993).

It is with such questions in mind that the fate of universities in the twenty-first century must be approached. Credible models of higher education for the future must build on, but also go beyond, an understanding of what shaped the universities in this century. Such models have to anticipate and help to shape the future.

Education and employment:
two contrasting views

That higher education has throughout the twentieth century slowly accommodated itself to waves of economic, social and technological change is not a matter of dispute. What is, however, contentious is the differing explanations offered for these socio-economic changes and what are thought to be appropriate responses from education. Two main explanations will now be compared. The common sense view, which Phillip Brown[2] and Richard Scase (1994) call 'the technocratic model' and which is presented in Figure 1.1, presents a dangerously oversimplified account of the relationships between employment and education.

Rapid technological change → Increasing skill levels → Expansion of HE/FE → Shift to learning society

Figure 1.1 Relationship between education and employment: the technocratic model.

The essential elements of this functionalist model are briefly described as follows: developments in technology, in methods of production and in the globalization of world trade, are said to require a more highly skilled workforce. Employers begin to apply pressure for educational standards to be improved. The outcome of this pressure can be seen in the government's first White Paper on competitiveness (HMSO 1994), which was subtitled *Helping Business to Win* and in which the Prime Minister, John Major, argued in the introduction that the skills of our young people 'will be the key to our future'. In the second White Paper on competitiveness, the main aim of the government in introducing the new National Targets for Education and Training is 'to improve the UK's international competitiveness by raising standards and attainment levels in education and training to world class levels' (HMSO 1995: 80). Hence, among many other measures, the massive expansion of higher and further education aims to supply the increased number of professionally trained and technically qualified workers which the modern economy claims to need. This argument takes one final step: the UK should become a learning society, and should develop 'a culture of continuing improvement [because] competitiveness is dynamic. We cannot ever afford to stand still. For as we change and innovate, the outside world also changes. And so the pressures continue' (HMSO 1994: 159). The key to sustainable economic prosperity is considered to be highly skilled workers who are also lifelong, flexible learners.

This argument could be used to justify a further expansion of higher and further education, but it is too one-sided: the interactions of physical and human capital have always been more complex, and are especially so in the new high-tech manufacturing industries, where the organization of work and the process of automation are both constantly employed to diminish dependence on skilled workers. For instance, Fujitsu, which produces micro-chips near Darlington, invested approximately £1 million in plant and equipment for each of the 500 jobs it originally created, and a further expansion (involving another 600 jobs) will again cost £1 million per job (Aviss 1995). Many thousands of the 140,000 unemployed in the North (*Labour Market Trends* March 1996) could, in fact, be trained to perform these jobs, but the region would still need 127 such plants to eradicate unemployment. The paradox of modern industry is that a strong manufacturing base is an essential precondition for long-term economic growth, but it does not create many jobs: so high, structural unemployment is likely to continue to coexist even with a high-tech, high-investment economy. Investment in education and training is a *necessary* but not a *sufficient* condition of sustained economic prosperity: the point is neatly captured in the phrase 'Let them eat skills.'

This exhortation is the title of an article by Douglas Noble, who argues that in the USA, as in Germany or the UK, 'there is a dire shortage of decent jobs, not a shortage of skilled labour . . . The wages and job security of those still employed are steadily eroding, as organised labour has been all but destroyed, and most new jobs are in the low-wage, temporary, part-time, service sector, requiring minimal skills' (Noble 1994: 22). The result may be a highly skilled elite and a growing army of the (at best) semi-skilled and expendable.

Such views are a necessary corrective to the current conventional wisdom, eloquently and influentially advocated on both sides of the Atlantic, which restricts attention to improving both the quality and quantity of the skills of the workforce. In the USA, Robert Reich (1993) has maintained that the only true competitive advantage lies in enhancing the skills and capacities, particularly of the new category of workers he calls 'symbolic analysts', who can identify, broker and solve new problems by manipulating symbols. In the UK, Sir Christopher Ball (1995) continues to proclaim that 'the quality of the education and training of the workforce is the single most important characteristic in determining economic competitiveness.' What is overlooked in their arguments is acknowledgement of the low demand for high-level skill in both countries. The work of Ewart Keep and Ken Mayhew is particularly associated with the view that significant sectors of the British economy 'are concentrating on low-specification, low-cost, standardised goods and services that create a weak demand for additional skills' (Keep and Mayhew 1995: 9). So additional public investment in higher and further education may only result in disappointment and frustration for future cohorts of graduates unless a means is found of increasing the demand for skills across the British economy.

Brown and Scase (1994) advance different reasons for rejecting the 'technocratic model' and they do so principally because it does not stand up to examination, either theoretically or empirically. On theoretical grounds, the 'technocratic model' is thought to be seriously deficient because it ignores 'the power play of competing vested interest groups [which] is vital to a full understanding of both educational change and the labour market' (Brown and Scase 1994: 17). In a similar vein, Stephen Ball (1993) concludes that the market reforms which have been implemented in British education are producing winners and losers; the winners tend to be middle-class families, who, through their knowledge of the system, are reasserting their advantages in education, while the losers tend to be working-class families, who so value their local community that they send their children to the nearest school rather than compete for places at 'successful' schools, which may be some miles away.

A model of social polarization, again based on Brown and Scase's original argument about social exclusion, has greater explanatory value than the 'technocratic model', and this alternative approach is presented in Figure 1.2. Support for this competing explanation comes from the empirical examination of the claim that there has been a general upskilling of the workforce. Duncan Gallie studied patterns of skill change in the UK and assessed the evidence for three competing claims: is the workforce being upskilled, deskilled or polarized? He concluded that 'the argument that is best supported is that of a polarization of skill experiences between classes . . . those that already had relatively high levels of skill witnessed an increase in their skill levels, while those with low levels of skill saw their skills stagnate' (Gallie 1994: 75).

Gallie's research suggests that two factors appear to be at work simultaneously. First, the skill requirements of some forms of work are rising sharply and are being extended to many more members of the workforce. At the same time, however, a deep class and gender divide in skill formation is taking place: 'there are also great differences in virtually every aspect of training and development between those in higher-level jobs and those in jobs at lower skill levels. There was a marked lack of provision for the one-third of employees with very low levels of qualification' (Gallie and White 1993: x).

The long controversy between upskilling or deskilling interpretations of the changing conditions of work has recently been reviewed and the conclusion reached that 'the nature and direction of skill change is unclear

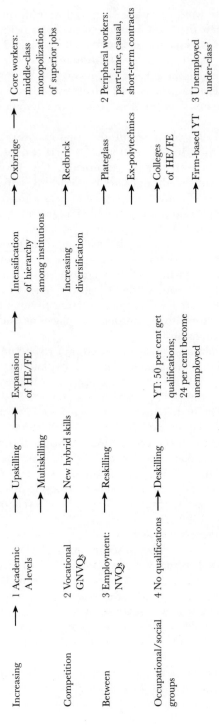

Figure 1.2 Relationship between education and employment: the social polarization model.

because there is no uniform effect' (Parsons and Marshall 1995: 7). Harry Braverman's (1974) well known thesis about the increasing degredation of work in the twentieth century finds only limited support, but Parsons and Marshall (1995: 15) add that 'many of the lower-skilled jobs . . . have been effectively de-skilled out of existence through process automation.' New hybrid combinations of skill across occupational boundaries were also found to coexist with upskilling, deskilling, reskilling and multiskilling: in short, the picture is becoming increasingly muddled, with traditional skill boundaries breaking down and with much still to be learned about the direction and detail of skill change.

Figure 1.2 is an attempt to capture some of the main features of this growing social polarization in contemporary Britain. So not only are the three pathways (A level, GNVQ and NVQ) in the national framework of qualifications listed, but a fourth pathway has been added, consisting of those who leave school with no or minimal qualifications. Sir Ron Dearing's review of qualifications for 16–19-year-olds shows that as many as 21 per cent of 17-year-olds were in neither education nor training (Dearing 1996: 5). This sizable minority has, in effect, precious little hope of ever becoming successful members of a global economy which celebrates and rewards a trained capacity to continue learning.

Moreover, the value of educational credentials begins to fall as a higher percentage of each generation achieves graduate status (up from 6 per cent in the early 1960s to almost 30 per cent in the early 1990s) when there is no corresponding expansion of elite jobs. Fred Hirsch accurately described one of the main consequences of this inflationary spiral which has taken off, with graduates reading for higher degrees to increase their chances of employment in a job market where the entry requirements are constantly rising: 'where educational expansion overcrowds superior positions as a whole . . . the effect will be to push competition by hitherto qualified applicants down the hierarchy of jobs: screening will be intensified at each level' (Hirsch 1977: 50). This process of 'downgrading' is already excluding many of the less qualified from the jobs they used to do.

Twenty years ago, Ronald Dore accurately described the paradox of the diploma disease, whereby 'the worse the educated unemployment situation gets and the more useless educational certificates become, the *stronger* grows the pressure for an expansion of educational facilities' (Dore 1976: 4; emphasis as in original).

So what is happening to those at the bottom of the system? Only 50 per cent of those who complete two years of Youth Training obtain a qualification and 24 per cent complete their training only to become unemployed (Maclagan 1996: 9). These percentages are the global national figures, which disguise both considerable regional variations (with far poorer outcomes in areas like Merseyside and the North-East which reflect the state of local labour markets) and high rates of early leaving: the national completion rate is 46 per cent (Dearing 1996: 13), with 25 per cent completing in Merseyside and 63 per cent in Hertfordshire. David Raffe and Paula

Surridge's review of the evidence about the participation in Britain of 16–18-year-olds in education fully endorses the alternative model:

> Britain may stabilise as a medium participation system in which participation and attainment are highly polarised. In this scenario a large proportion of the age group will graduate from higher education but few will leave with intermediate qualifications. A large minority will continue to leave early, or will stay on but achieve little of value; this minority will be at greatest risk of unemployment and other disadvantage.
>
> (Raffe and Surridge 1995: 3)

The expansion of the higher and further education sectors and the market in education have also brought in their train an increasing diversification and an intensification of the hierarchy among institutions, because, just as with the school system, markets require variety and choice. In the words of A. H. Halsey (1995: 31), 'In Britain the paradoxical outcome has been a more elaborate pyramid of prestige, with Oxford and Cambridge never more securely placed at the apex on the basis of academic merit while retaining more sumptuous amenities and superior social connections.' Britain's blue chip companies are not, of course, even-handed in the universities they are prepared to recruit graduates from, with the result that more than 20 per cent of graduates from some of the 'new' universities are still unemployed six months after graduation. The unemployment rate for new graduates in the system as a whole was 11 per cent in 1993.

The final column of Figure 1.2 summarizes the alternative thesis: British society is polarizing and three main groups can be discerned. Will Hutton (1995: 105) labels the UK 'the thirty, thirty, forty society', where the bottom 30 per cent are the disadvantaged (unemployed or economically inactive), the next 30 per cent are the marginalized and the insecure, and the final 40 per cent are the privileged in full-time jobs but with less security than in the recent past. The most anxious of all are those who have cause to fear that they may slip into a lower category. If this model of social and economic polarization is a reasonably accurate description of some of the main trends in the UK, then future plans for higher and further education will have to take account of it. A useful start would be for both sectors to acknowledge openly that, for reasons of financial exigency, their employment policies have been contributing to the divisions in society by creating armies of part-time, casual teaching staff, predominantly women, on short-time contracts, who receive little or no staff development or training.[3] Such measures help large institutions to cope with sudden fluctuations in funding, but a temporary expedient has become standard procedure, raising moral as well as financial questions about its continued use.

Evidence to support a thesis of polarization in the UK has been accumulating for years but this is not the place for a comprehensive review; instead, two powerful, detailed and representative studies will be briefly referred to. First, the Joseph Rowntree Foundation published in February 1995 a two volume report, entitled *Inquiry into Income and Wealth*. Some of the key findings from the report can be summarized as follows.

• Income inequality in the UK grew very rapidly between 1977 and 1990 and reached the highest level recorded since the Second World War.
• It might, however, be argued that this finding is simply reflecting an international trend, whereby all nations are affected by global markets, which domestic policy can do little to mitigate. The report refutes this interpretation by showing that, apart from New Zealand, the UK was exceptional in the pace and extent of the increase in inequality in the 1980s. There has been no general trend towards greater inequality.
• In the period 1975–93, a growing polarization took place in the UK between 'work rich' and 'work poor' households. The proportion of two adult households where both adults were earners rose from 51 to 60 per cent, while the proportion with no earner rose from 3 to 11 per cent.
• Polarization between deprived and affluent neighbourhoods gradually increased during the 1980s. Poverty is becoming concentrated on 'peripheral' council housing estates, which have been called 'landscapes of despair' (Donnison 1994: 20).
• Wealth has not 'trickled down' from the richest section of society. Over the period 1979–92 the poorest 20–30 per cent of the population did not benefit from economic growth, and children are disproportionately represented in this group. More specifically, the wages of the bottom 10 per cent hardly changed in real terms, while those of the top 10 per cent rose by 50 per cent.

The second study supports the basic findings of the Rowntree Report. David Gordon and Ray Forrest (1995: 5) have produced an atlas of some of the key social and economic divisions in England based on the 1991 Census, and after measuring and mapping deprivation in three different ways, they conclude as follows: 'Poverty had become so widespread in England by 1991, and its manifestations were so varied, that the same broad patterns can be discerned almost irrespective of the methods used to measure it. To put it bluntly, when there is a lot of poverty it becomes relatively easy to measure.' More to our present purpose, their maps and charts indicate the spatial concentration of the highly educated, with the district of the City of London having the highest proportion of adult residents with degrees (29.9 per cent), while the district of Barking and Dagenham was at the other end of the scale, with only 1.5 per cent with degrees (Gordon and Forrest 1995: 69). The message of their 36 maps and charts is the same: 'This atlas provides ample evidence for the existence of social polarisation with strong spatial characteristics. Problems of unemployment, poverty and ill health are concentrated in the major cities, the depressed industrial north and in the forgotten corners of England. By contrast, areas of affluence and privilege are found in the extended suburban south east. These patterns suggest a country divided, rather than at ease with itself' (p. 9).

This is the social context within which new models of higher and further education need urgently to be developed: existing divisions appear to be deepening and new divisions are also being created. In response, universities need to renegotiate their relations with their local communities and be differentially funded to take account of varying regional needs. And if evidence continues to mount of social polarization, then the case for increasing the proportion of young people entering higher education will have to be considered alongside other options for investment in education. Keep and Mayhew (1995: 94) have, for instance, argued that public money, spent on basic skills training, and on retraining the adult unemployed and the peripheral workforce, 'would probably produce a significantly higher social rate of return than any additional expansion of undergraduate provision.' The three options to which they accord priority would benefit 'those who are currently among the most disadvantaged in the labour market, and whose educational and training problems, not least in terms of consequent unemployment, impose very significant social and economic costs on society as a whole' (p. 93). It is now widely argued that a prosperous economy and a just and cohesive society are not conflicting but complementary objectives: here is an opportunity to turn that slogan into reality.

A possible response could, however, be: 'Why should higher education concern itself with such inequalities?' We would counter that the claims which academics make for special treatment from society (e.g. the intellectual space and freedom to develop new ideas and to criticize the existing order) carry with them the responsibility to have a care for *all* members of that society, and especially for the disadvantaged. The contract, then, between higher education and society offers special privileges to academics in return for a commitment to the democratic health and progress of that society. The main contribution which universities can make to social stability is to be engaged in the life of their local communities, to research their most pressing problems and to offer constructive, if at times challenging, ways forward. All debates about the future of higher education are inseparable from debates about the future of society.

The challenges facing higher education

The challenges facing higher education are formidable and, as Robin Middlehurst points out in Chapter 3, if the universities' response is low-level, incremental improvement, it may prove 'insufficient and possibly dangerous': what is needed is nothing less than a transformation of the system. Nine key issues are briefly introduced below and are then developed in a variety of ways in subsequent chapters to offer the reader a choice of competing visions for the future.

First, thirty years after the Robbins Report, the technological, social, economic and intellectual contexts have changed so markedly that a new vision of higher education needs to be developed. Existing models of higher education have been extensively criticized and Tapper and Salter (1992:

246) have claimed that 'the most profound criticism of the universities has been their failure to create their own vision of the future.' This book is a direct response to their criticism, and in the chapters by Stephen McNair, David Robertson, Robin Middlehurst, Ronald Barnett, Chris Duke and the final chapter by Bill Williamson and Frank Coffield, different visions of the future for higher education are offered as a contribution to the public debate.

Second, a national strategy for industry needs to be developed at the same time as a new coherent policy for education and training, *and the two need to be coordinated.* Sufficient has been said earlier about investment in education being a necessary but not a sufficient condition for economic prosperity. Employers need to be constantly nudged up the productivity escalator to produce higher quality goods and services so that the talents developed through the rapid expansion of higher and further education are put to productive use. The role of the state is critical here to ensure that investment in industry, in innovation and in the necessary economic and technical infrastructure is integrated with investment in education and training.

Ashton and Sung (1994: 31) argue that the South-east Asian economies, and particularly Singapore, are operating a new model of skill formation which may be superior to British, German or Japanese models, in that the state intervenes 'to direct, shape and enhance the skill base of the society'. The Singaporean system is best conceptualized *not* as central planning but as 'a new form of government intervention . . . in which the government has sought to understand the operation of market forces and use them to realise its political objectives' (Ashton and Sung 1997: 14). A levy was imposed, for example, on companies with low-paid labour to encourage them to move out of low value-added production. As long as the Singaporean model is confined to its own population of three million, it will not pose a major threat to European economies; but if, as seems likely, that model is successfully adopted by Taiwan, South Korea, Malaysia and, heaven forbid, China, then the current British government policy of international competitiveness based on an unregulated market will be cruelly exposed.

Third, a central advisory policy unit should be established to offer advice to government on the future of higher education and to sharpen up policy options on priorities, funding, student support and the development of human resource for the academic profession. When this proposal was first published (Coffield 1995), the main leader in the *Times Higher Education Supplement* (20 October 1995) found it 'alarming' and completely misread the recommendation as suggesting that 'change should be forcibly imposed' by such an agency. But the original proposal advocated the development of policy and not control, and used the language of influence, encouragement and incentives as follows: 'Central planning must allow for creativity and diversity when determining priorities and funding; and institutional autonomy must respond to national needs and policies while defending internal democracy and disinterested criticism' (Coffield 1995: 20). Balancing conflicting objectives is a delicate but not impossible task and institutions are likely to develop in the search for a dynamic equilibrium.

Fourth, one of the unexpected consequences of the expansion of higher education is that universities are no longer the main producers of knowledge in modern societies – able graduates now create new scientific, social and cultural knowledge in a wide variety of research centres and industrial laboratories which are independent of universities. Michael Gibbons and his colleagues (1994) have described the emergence of a new mode of knowledge production, which they label mode 2 to distinguish it from the traditional, disciplinary methods of creating new knowledge, which they term mode 1. The characteristic features of mode 2 are that knowledge is produced in the context of application; it is transdisciplinary, heterogeneous, transient and non-hierarchical (because based on collaborative, horizontal relationships); it is less institutionally based, is socially accountable and reflexive, and employs different criteria of quality control.

The implications of a new research paradigm are only now beginning to be felt in universities, which 'will need a new management style, which can cope with permeable boundaries between institutions' (Gibbons *et al.* 1994: 155), new career patterns for academics and new forms of partnership with other knowledge producers, both local and international.

Fifth, the structure of power within universities will need to be rethought if the traditional principle within British universities of self-government by academics themselves is to be preserved. In too many institutions of higher and further education, the new managerialism has deliberately dismantled the mechanisms of participative democracy, so that, for example, councils and governing bodies which should be acting as a check on executive power have been emasculated. As a result, lack of trust in senior management is now endemic throughout higher and further education: the ties of loyalty which used to bind professionals to their institution have been broken; staff remain committed to their students and to their discipline but are openly contemptuous of incompetent and punitive management. Academics in the UK are expected to 'empower' their students by passing the responsibility for learning over to the learners and to provide them with practical experience of active citizenship in a democratic society, yet they themselves find fewer and fewer opportunities to engage in participative decision-making within their own organizations. To paraphrase a remark of Martin Luther's, the surprise is not that many employees become over-committed to their work but rather that employers and organizations receive much more than they deserve.[4] Democratic self-government is not so much an expensive self-indulgence as the necessary safeguard of the critical space academics need both to question society and to articulate different visions of that society – a main theme of the final chapter.

The case for principled dissent must be argued anew because, as A. J. P. Taylor asserted in a famous passage, dissent transcends criticism and contains the seeds of change: 'Conformity may give you a quiet life; it may even bring you to a University Chair. But all change in history, all advance, comes from the nonconformists. If there had been no trouble-makers, no Dissenters, we should still be living in caves' (Taylor 1993: 14). The suppression of dissent in Nazi Germany led quickly to intellectual stagnation in the universities; for Hitler, 'scientific objectivity was a slogan coined by the professors simply in order to escape from the necessary supervision by the power of the state' (Fest 1979: 388).

Sixth, the catchment area of many universities is shrinking and shrinking fast, but their relationships with the local community are likely to be 'a patchwork quilt of overlapping and uncoordinated initiatives . . . [and] what is missing is an overall vision of how this effort can be linked to the economic regeneration' of the locality (Goddard 1993: 7–8). As with wealth and the poor, the 'trickle down' theory of benefits accruing to local communities from institutions of higher and further education does not work in practice unless specific mechanisms are put in place and regularly evaluated. Two examples are worth quoting. In California, structures of opportunity have been created which link together into one coordinated system the community college, the state university and the elite University of California, so that anyone who enters a local college can move steadily upwards and join an internationally renowned university: in this way, equity and excellence are reconciled (see OECD 1990). In the UK similar networks are being established, as Chris Duke explains in Chapter 4 in relation to the University of Warwick and local further education colleges.

Seventh, the global market is only now beginning to affect the international role of universities; but, for instance, developments in information technology now make it possible for prospective MBA students in Fiji to choose to study via interactive techniques in an elite university in the USA or in the UK rather than physically attend their local University of the South Pacific. An international market in curricula and in academic 'stars' has already begun, and international competition among elite universities will be added to national evaluations such as the Research Assessment Exercise. Moreover, European programmes such as Socrates and Leonardo are likely to have marked effects on the mobility of students, staff and skilled workers. In fewer than ten years the number of students participating in the Erasmus Programme grew from 3000 to 170,000, and some students now arrive at university with the expectation that they will study in another European country as part of their initial degree (European Commission 1996: 81).

Eighth, twenty-five years ago Edgar Faure proposed that lifelong education should become 'the master concept of educational policies in the years to come' (Faure *et al.* 1972: 181). Lifelong learning has taken off within the universities as the steep rise of 115 per cent since the mid-1980s (Burgess 1996) in the number of postgraduate students testifies, but the government's consultation document on lifetime learning (DfEE 1995) is seriously deficient, dependent as it is on *individuals* taking responsibility for learning throughout their lives. Most of the lifetime learning targets for the year 2000 are likely to be met with the major exception of the target requiring *organizations* to be recognized as 'Investors in People'. Seventy per cent of all firms with 200 or more employees and 35 per cent of those employing 50 or more constitute the target, but currently only 8 per cent of the larger organizations and only 5 per cent of the smaller have qualified. As with the universities, institutional rather than individual reform has to be the main focus of policy. And if the universities were to transform themselves in the ways outlined in this volume, they could become *the* institutions which usher in a learning society.

The competence-based approach to initial professional training and to continuing professional development is meanwhile gaining in momentum despite a barrage of criticism (e.g. Hyland 1994; Bates 1995), and is chang- ing both teaching and assessment practices in those areas of higher edu- cation where it has been introduced. In Australia, for example, twenty professions are currently developing competence standards with funds from government, but with a more sophisticated concept of competence than that employed by the National Council for Vocational Qualifications in England (see Hager and Gonczi 1996: 246).

Universities currently provide opportunities for graduates to read for higher degrees or to be updated professionally, but they have not incorpor- ated the concept of lifelong learning into undergraduate degrees. Malcolm Skilbeck has, for instance, pointed to a missing dimension in undergradu- ate education – the need to 'develop a conception of education in which undergraduate studies are an integral part of a continuing sequence of learning across the whole life span' (Skilbeck 1996).

Ninth, the transformations of higher education for which we argue will not succeed without major financial support from the state; and if its mis- sion is extended to meet the new goals, purposes and challenges listed, then resources commensurate with these objectives have to be made avail- able. What is obvious is that, without such funding, no new developments are possible and that maintaining present activities is put at risk by the deep cuts in total expenditure and in capital spending announced in the Chan- cellor's budget in November 1995. The role of the state remains central to determining the shape, size and purposes of higher education in any ad- vanced, industrial country.

It remains true that funding a mass system of higher education will also depend upon making more effective and more equitable use of resources as well as increasing them. For example, the state could finance for all a shorter initial experience of higher education (a two-year foundation de- gree) and leave individuals, helped by a graduate contribution scheme, to meet the costs of further qualifications. Stephen McNair ends Chapter 6 by proposing such a radical solution, and the strengths and weaknesses of his proposal deserve much closer attention than they have yet received by academics. Moreover, a significant advance towards the learning society would be made by extending the public funding of tuition costs to all part- time students; in this way the system would be enticed away from its con- centration on full-time study to embrace part-time education, distance and lifelong learning. A fundamental reform of the funding of tuition fees and student maintenance, involving a redistribution of the costs of higher education among the beneficiaries, needs to be part of a new strategic plan for higher education. The divisive issues of determining priorities, introducing greater funding differentials to increase the proportion of science and engineering students and concentrating research (particularly in the high-cost areas within science) in high-quality institutions have all still to be faced.

This concentration on the challenges confronting higher education should not be interpreted as an unwillingness to appreciate the solid and substantial successes which the system has also enjoyed. It is simply that the achievements (e.g. low drop-out rates; comparatively short, cost-effective first degrees; increases in foreign students; dramatic expansion from an elite to a mass system; and innovations in open and distance leaning) have been discussed elsewhere (see Coffield 1995: 7ff). It is also tempting to overstate the limitations of the present model as Lord Dahrendorf (1995: 17) has done with his provocative question: 'Are universities among the great achievements of the 20th century which the 21st is not going to see?' The data so far are against him, for, as Stephen McNair rightly points out in Chapter 6, 'almost the only kind of organization which has grown in size is the university' – and particularly central administration within each institution. Lord Dahrendorf is on firmer ground when he criticizes the intellectual rigidities of the subject disciplines – 'the guild-like nature of these communities can positively block new insights' (p. 12). Managing change in departments, which in Kenneth Edwards's (1994: 143) phrase are 'loose confederations of academics', should not, however, be underestimated. What we have learned is that the model of change which has been borrowed from industrial and commercial organizations and imposed on universities is not appropriate to the nature of work in higher education.

Conclusion

This chapter has sought to understand higher education in four ways.

- By examining the new language from industry, which, if not challenged, will fashion a very different future for universities and will undermine the legitimate role of universities in exploring critically different options for the future.
- By arguing that universities need to know their own history and use an honest evaluation of their successes and failures to construct their own models of the future; indeed, universities in democratic societies have a responsibility so to act, not least because their own futures are inseparable from those of the societies they serve.
- By proposing that social and economic polarization in the UK should be tackled before higher education is expanded further; universities will be diminished and perhaps even damaged if they ignore the widening gulf between different sections of society.

- By listing the main challenges facing the system, which together require universities to change fundamentally and not just incrementally.

These considerations suggest that the purposes of higher education also need to be re-examined, and that is the final task of this introduction.

Richard Hoggart has argued that universities advance knowledge, educate clever people to pursue the same end, but are also 'places in which people are made aware of the moral situation of their disciplines, are led to question the terms of life offered by their societies and those they have so far proposed for themselves' (Hoggart 1982: 70).

The terms of life offered to the new classes in society – the privileged 'core' workers, the insecure 'peripheral' workers and the disadvantaged at the bottom of the pile – are now so different that a main task has become how to hold society together. As the forces of polarization and exclusion intensify, the sense of social solidarity felt by the 'core' workers towards their fellow citizens will be tested to the full. The response to the 'centrifugal forces of the global economy which tear at the ties binding citizens together' (Reich 1993: 3) must surely be to cultivate all the centripetal forces of social cohesion.

A start would be made by reinterpreting progressive income tax, not as a burden on enterprise, but as a means of promoting social justice. We also need to strengthen all the intermediate institutions of civil society, those institutions capable of standing up to the power of the state and of involving individuals in purposes greater than their own. Active citizenship could help to counteract the cult of competitive individualism. It is probably true, as Geoff Mulgan (1996) reminds us, that 'for most people a job is a far more important symbol of citizenship even than a vote or constitutional rights', but the dogmatic application of the market principle is undermining this social order.

Hierarchy and deference provided much of the social cement in the past but are out of place in an open, egalitarian and pluralistic society. The education system has a contribution to make to social cohesion and early versions of the National Curriculum for 5–16-year-olds held out hope that cross-curricular themes would include education for citizenship, but the 1994 Dearing review of the curriculum omitted any mention of these themes. Terry McLaughlin (1992) has pleaded for a wide-ranging national debate about the character of education for citizenship, a 'maximal' interpretation of which would emphasize critical understanding and questioning on the part of students.

The case for civic education in schools has been well made by David Hargreaves (1994: 31), who wishes 'to ensure that people with different moral, religious and ethical values as well as social, cultural and linguistic traditions can live together with a degree of harmony'. It is highly likely that in universities, under pressure from industrialists, the Dearing Committee of Inquiry will recommend that all future students should follow courses in the 'core' skills of literacy, numeracy and information technology, but these alone will not deepen their understanding of society. If even part of the rhetoric about a second industrial revolution having dawned is true, then students need to be intellectually and socially prepared to manage periods of work and non-work and to cope with perpetual change. Higher education must not be reduced to the means of supplying industry with technically competent but socially illiterate graduates; it must develop people capable of creating and shaping a more prosperous, a more just and a more integrated society.

One of the four aims of higher education, according to the Robbins Report, was 'the transmission of a common culture and common standards of citizenship' (Committee on Higher Education 1963: 7). Few now believe in a common culture for universities to transmit, but higher education and British society could be transformed and renewed by a commitment to membership of a society of citizens, not merely membership of an association of consumers. In particular, David Robertson in Chapter 5 proposes the development of *internal citizenship* for all categories of university staff *and* students, 'which goes beyond the public relations gimmicks of student charters'.

There are educational resources which could be effectively mobilized in the cause of social solidarity, but, if social scientists have learned anything in the period since the publication of the Robbins Report in 1963, it is that educational efforts on their own are not sufficient and may be in fact a substitute for more radical economic, political and institutional reform. Brown and Lauder (1996: 20) clearly enunciate the central question which all advanced, industrial societies must now confront: 'how to organise the competition for a livelihood in such a way that a genuinely equal opportunity is available to all.' The following chapters show in detail how the purposes and practices of higher education in the UK need to be transformed before a genuinely equal opportunity is available to all British citizens. We invite the Dearing Committe of Inquiry to agree with David Robertson (in this volume) that the new vision for higher education 'must involve a fundamental commitment to social justice and an acceptance that the pursuit of social justice is an arm of national effectiveness'; if the Committee does not agree, then it must present its own vision of higher education. Let the debate begin![5]

Notes

1. The same decisive shift in language and in values is taking place in schools, where headteachers seek to cope with the new vocabulary of management by 'becoming bilingual or learning to talk management' (Gewirtz *et al.* 1995: 98).
2. The main author of this chapter, Frank Coffield, is grateful for the stimulus provided by the arguments presented by Phillip Brown and Richard Scase and freely acknowledges them as the source of the ideas presented here. A comparison, however, of the two accounts will show that the original argument has been considerably elaborated and developed.

3. One estimate puts the number of university-based researchers on short-term contracts at some 18,000 in 1995 (see SET Forum 1995: 25).
4. John Osborne (1965: 41) in his play gives the following lines to Martin Luther: 'Churches, kings and fathers – why do they ask so much, and why do they all of them get so much more than they deserve?'
5. Madeleine Atkins, Bruce Carrington, Tony Edwards, Jackson Hall and Richard Smith are all thanked for their perceptive comments on an earlier draft of this chapter.

References

Annan, N. (1990) *Our Age: the Generation that Made Post-war Britain.* London, Fontana.
Ashton, D. and Green, F. (1996) *Education, Training and the Global Economy.* Cheltenham, Edward Elgar.
Ashton, D. and Sung, J. (1994) The state, education and training systems and economic development: a new East Asia model? Leicester University Centre for Labour Market Studies.
Ashton, D. and Sung, J. (1997) Education, skill formation and economic development: the Singaporean approach', forthcoming.
Aviss, L. (1995) Micro chips or pommes frites – can you tell them apart? Lecture at conference, 'Education and Training for the Future Labour Markets of Europe', Durham University, 22 September.
Ball, Sir Christopher (1995) Developing the learning society, Presidential address, North of England Conference, York University, 4 January.
Ball, S. (1993) Education markets, choice and social class: the market as a class strategy in the UK and the USA, *British Journal of Sociology of Education,* 14(1), 3–19.
Barnett, R. (1993) *The Idea of Higher Education.* Buckingham, Open University Press/SRHE.
Bates, I. (1995) The competence movement: conceptualising recent research, *Studies in Science Education,* 25, 39–68.
Becher, T. (1989) *Academic Tribes and Territories: Intellectual Enquiry and the Culture of Disciplines.* Milton Keynes, Open University Press/SRHE.
Beck, U. (1992) *Risk Society: towards a New Modernity.* London, Sage.
Bracher, K. D. (1970) *The German Dictatorship: the Origins, Structure and Consequences of National Socialism.* Harmondsworth, Penguin.
Braverman, H. (1974) *Labor and Monopoly Capital: the Degradation of Work in the Twentieth Century.* New York, Monthly Review Press.
Brown, P. and Lauder, H. (1996) Education, globalisation and economic development, *Journal of Education Policy,* 11(1), 1–25.
Brown, P. and Scase, R. (1994) *Higher Education and Corporate Realities: Class, Culture and the Decline of Graduate Careers.* London, University College London Press.
Burgess, R. G. (1996) Trends and developments in postgraduate education and training the UK, *Journal of Education Policy,* 1(1), 125–32.
Coffield, F. (ed.) (1995) *Higher Education in a Learning Society.* Durham, School of Education for DfEE/ESRC/HEFCE.
Committee on Higher Education (1963) *Higher Education.* London, HMSO Cmnd 2154 (the Robbins Report).
CVCP (1995) *Part-time Study in Higher Education.* London, CVCP Briefing Note.

Dahrendorf, Lord (1995) *Whither Social Sciences?* 6th ESRC Annual Lecture. Swindon, ESRC.

Dearing, Sir Ron (1994) *The National Curriculum and Its Assessment.* Final Report. London, SCAA.

Dearing, Sir Ron (1996) *Review of Qualifications for 16–19 Year Olds.* Summary Report. London, SCAA.

Department for Education and Employment (1995) *Lifetime Learning: a Consultation Document.* London, HMSO.

Donnison, D. (1994) *Act Local: Social Justice from the Bottom Up.* London, IPPR.

Dore, R. (1976) *The Diploma Disease: Education, Qualification and Development.* London, Allen and Unwin.

Edwards, K. (1994) Focusing the university: the changing role of the vice-chancellor, in S. Weil (ed.) *Introducing Change from the Top in Universities and Colleges.* London, Kogan Page.

European Commission (1996) *Teaching and Learning: towards the Learning Society.* White Paper on Education and Training. Luxembourg, Office for Official Publications of the EC.

Faure, E. *et al.* (1972) *Learning to Be: the World of Education Today and Tomorrow.* Paris, UNESCO.

Fest, J. (1979) *The Face of the Third Reich.* Harmondsworth, Penguin.

Finger, M. (1995) Adult education and society today, *International Journal of Lifelong Learning,* 14(2), 110–20.

Gallie, D. (1994) Patterns of skill change: upskilling, deskilling or polarisation?, in R. Penn, M. Rose and J. Rubery (eds) *Skill and Occupation Change.* Oxford, Oxford University Press.

Gallie, D. and White, M. (1993) *Employee Commitment and the Skills Revolution.* London, Policy Studies Institute.

Gellert, C. (1993) *Higher Education in Europe.* London, Jessica Kingsley.

Gewirtz, S., Ball, S. J. and Bowe, R. (1995) *Markets, Choice and Equity in Education.* Buckingham, Open University Press.

Gibbons, M. *et al.* (1994) *The New Production of Knowledge: the Dynamics of Science and Research in Contemporary Societies.* London, Sage.

Goddard, J. (1993) The university and the technopolis, paper presented to 15th Quintennial Congress of the Commonwealth Universities, Swansea.

Gordon, D. and Forrest, R. (1995) *People and Places 2: Social and Economic Distinctions in England.* Bristol, School for Advanced Urban Studies.

Hager, P. and Gonczi, A. (1996) Professions and competencies, in R. Edwards, A. Hanson and P. Raggatt (eds) *Boundaries of Adult Learning.* London, Routledge for Open University, 246–60.

Halsey, A. H. (1995) Dons' decline reviewed, in F. Coffield (ed.) *Higher Education in a Learning Society.* Durham, Durham University School of Education for DfEE, ESRC and HEFCE.

Hargreaves, D. (1994) *The Mosaic of Learning: Schools and Teachers for the Next Century.* London, Demos.

Havel, V. (1987) *Living within Truth.* London, Faber and Faber.

Hirsch, F. (1977) *Social Limits to Growth.* London, Routledge and Kegan Paul.

HMSO (1994) *Competitiveness: Helping Business to Win.* Cm. 2563. London, HMSO.

HMSO (1995) *Competitiveness: Forging Ahead.* Cm. 2867. London, HMSO.

Hobsbawm, E. (1994) *Age of Extremes: the Short Twentieth Century, 1914–1991.* London, Michael Joseph.

Hoggart, R. (1982) *An English Temper: Essays on Education, Culture and Communications*. London, Chatto and Windus.

Hutton, W. (1995) *The State We're In*. London, Jonathan Cape.

Hyland, T. (1994) *Competence, Education and NVQs: Dissenting Perspectives*. London, Cassell.

Keegan, D. (ed.) (1994) *Otto Peters on Distance Education: the Industrialisation of Teaching and Learning*. London, Routledge.

Keep, E. and Mayhew, K. (1995) Training policy for competitiveness – time for a fresh perspective?, in H. Metcalf (ed.) *Future Skill Demand and Supply*. London, PSI.

Laquer, W. (1982) *Europe Since Hitler: the Rebirth of Europe*. Harmondsworth, Penguin.

Maclagan, Z. (1996) YT leavers survey, *Working Brief*, 72, 9–11.

McLaughlin, T. H. (1992) Citizenship, diversity and education: a philosophical perspective, *Journal of Moral Education*, 21(3), 235–50.

Mamet, D. (1993) *Oleanna*. London, Methuen.

Middlehurst, R. (1993) *Leading Academics*. Buckingham, Open University Press/SRHE.

Mulgan, G. (1996) Article in *The Guardian*, 30 January.

Noble, D. (1994) Let them eat skills, *The Review of Education, Pedagogy, Cultural Studies*, 16(1), 15–29.

OECD (1990) *Higher Education in California*. Paris, OECD.

Osborne, J. (1965) *Luther*. London, Faber and Faber.

Parsons, D. and Marshall, V. (1995) *Skills, Qualifications and Utilisation: a Research Review*, Research Series No. 67. Sheffield, DfEE.

Poerksen, U. (1995) *Plastic Words: the Tyranny of a Modular Language*. Philadelphia, Pennsylvania State University Press.

Raffe, D. (1992) Beyond the 'mixed model': social research and the case for reform of 16–18 education in Britain, in C. Crouch and A. Heath (eds) *Social Research and Social Reform: Essays in Honour of A. H. Halsey*. Oxford, Clarendon.

Raffe, D. and Surridge, P. (1995) More of the same? Participation of 16–18 year olds in education. London, National Commission on Education, briefing paper, new series no. 6.

Reich, R. B. (1993) *The Work of Nations*. London, Simon & Schuster.

Rowntree, Joseph Foundation (1995) *Inquiry into Income and Wealth*. York, Rowntree Foundation.

Scott, P. (1995) *The Meanings of Mass Higher Education*. Buckingham, Open University Press/SRHE.

SET Forum (1995) *Shaping the Future: a Policy for Science, Engineering and Technology*. Milton Keynes, Open University.

Skilbeck, M. (1996) Lifelong learning – a missing dimension in undergraduate education, in F. Coffield (ed.) forthcoming.

Tapper, T. and Salter, B. (1992) *Oxford, Cambridge and the Changing Idea of the University: the Challenge to Donnish Domination*. Buckingham, Open University Press/SRHE.

Taylor, A. J. P. (1993) *The Troublemakers*. London, Pimlico.

2

Beyond Competence

Ronald Barnett

Introduction

Competence has recently entered the language of higher education in the UK. Through the work of the National Council for Vocational Qualifications (NCVQ), it may seem to offer an organizing principle for the reform of the curriculum and the educational experience we offer students. The world of work clearly requires competent people. Very well: let us design our curricula so that they are producing graduates with the proper competences for the workplace. Learning, accordingly, should be competency based.

In this chapter, I do not propose to evaluate this approach as such. That kind of critique has been offered elsewhere (Hyland 1994). Instead, I want to offer a larger canvas and do two things. First, I shall suggest that the idea of competence is nothing new in higher education. What is new is the particular idea of competence with which we are now confronted. In the past, education in our universities has been dominated by a notion of academic competence. That notion sees competence – even if the term was not used – as the capacity to see the world and to engage with it through one or more of the academic disciplines. Competence here has been understood to be the capacity to engage in a particular cognitive tradition, a conversation – as Oakeshott put it – of a particular kind (Fuller 1989). Now, we are seeing efforts to replace that idea of competence with another oriented towards the world of work. We have, therefore, not one but two rival versions of competence in the academy. It will be the elucidation of the characteristics and differences of these two versions of competence that will occupy much of our attention here.

Second, I want to put that exploration in a wider context still. The competency movement, I shall argue, is to be understood as part of larger social, economic and cognitive changes. It indicates a profound shift in the way in which we seek to know the world, especially in our evaluations of what counts as knowledge and truth. It is a sign that our social epistemologies are dynamic and are currently undergoing a significant change. But, in turn, these changes have to be understood within a larger context of economic change, of social change and, in turn, of changes in the relationship of education to work and society. And, in turn, these larger changes are having an impact on the relationships between higher education and society.

In summary, therefore, there are two arguments in this chapter; they are related but work on different levels. First, in higher education in the UK, we are faced with two rival versions of competence and we are seeing a move from one to the other, from an academic version of competence to a more operational definition. Second, this contest has to be seen as part of a changing set of relationships between knowledge, higher education and society. In that dynamic, we are witnessing a transformation in modern society as to what counts as worthwhile knowledge and, in particular, from contemplative to performative ways of knowing. I shall end, however, by suggesting that neither of the dominant alternative forms of knowing or of our aims in higher education are appropriate to the challenges of our modern age and that we require quite different ways both of conceiving of the world and of conducting our higher educational practices.

Knowledge, higher education and society

Any serious understanding of the educational experience we offer students has to be placed in the context of a wider sense of the changing relationships between knowledge, higher education and society. Higher education is a particularly social institution, established by and called upon by society to perform certain functions; and the balance of that relationship – between higher education and society – has, over the centuries, produced different definitions of education and knowing which are to be put the way of the students.

Universities were a creation of medieval society. There was no grand plan: the arrival of any particular university was the outcome of particular events, geography and chance. Oxford could have been Reading; Cambridge could have been Stamford. Nor were universities born fully fledged, but developed over some time to take the organizational form which in turn was to last several hundred years. The *universitas* – a grouping of scholars – eventually became a *studium generale*, a university recognized by King and Pope; and was granted considerable privileges in return for educating what were often the sons of relatively poor people. Themes of autonomy, privilege, equity, educational service, community and state recognition were all present, even from their early beginnings. The universities were not insignificant, then, in the medieval landscape.

For our purposes, certain key features stand out in comparing the medieval universities to those of modern society. First, the medieval universities collectively constituted a relatively modest institution in what was a rural traditional society; they were really on the fringe of things. Second, despite their relative marginality, their function of providing an educated stratum, in command of texts, language and rhetoric, was significant in that they were able to monopolize the definitions of worthwhile knowing. They were the epistemological guardians. Third, being educated, being literate and having attended a university was highly unusual (Gellner 1991). In such a society, where the mass of the people were illiterate, the function of the university was clear: to produce literate persons. All three conditions of the medieval university – of social significance, of epistemological monopoly and of educational supremacy – are now challenged in modern society.

We cannot understand modern society without giving a central place to the university. There is, however, an ambiguity at work. On the one hand, higher education has grown, has become massified and has become a state system. On the other hand, the former monopoly over the definitions of knowledge which the clerks enjoyed has vanished. And this change is seen in two ways. First, modern society is forming its own views as to what is to count as knowledge. Today, it dismisses contemplative knowledge, knowledge which brings personal understanding, even knowledge which offers truth. Now, it wants knowledge which is going to have demonstrable effects on the world, which is going to improve economic competitiveness and which is going to enhance personal effectiveness. In the process, our sense of what is to count as knowledge and truth changes; and the university is asked to take those new definitions on board.

Second, in the knowledge society, saturated with professional action, organizational and economic challenge, new sites of knowledge production emerge. Knowledge is produced in and through action; in the solving of organizational and technological problems; and in the generation of new social arrangements. This is not traditional propositional knowledge but is a different form of knowledge; from mode 1 to mode 2 knowledge, as it has recently been suggested (Gibbons *et al.* 1994).

In all three of its basic conditions, then, the relationships between higher education, knowledge and society are changing profoundly. First, higher education has become pivotal, and has grown enormously in size; and this is a recent phenomenon. Second, the universities have lost their monopoly over the definitions and, indeed, the production of knowledge (Hague 1991). Third, in the modern society everyone is literate (more or less).

Higher education, knowledge and society, therefore, are entering a new configuration. Crudely, the changes sketched out here take this form: a shift from

Higher education → knowledge → society

to

Society → knowledge → higher education

Until relatively recently, the academic class imposed its own definitions of knowledge on society, especially through its educative function. Now society is contesting those definitions of knowledge, is expressing its dissatisfaction with them and is seeking to have its own much more operational and instrumental definitions of knowledge taken up by higher education. The wider society, especially but not only in the form of the state, looks to impose its definitions of knowledge on the academy and to see them shaping the student experience. In short, we are seeing a complete inversion of the relationships between knowledge, higher education and society.

These are, of course, tendencies. No overnight wholesale change can seriously be posited. It is not being suggested that universities have lost their autonomy and have had, say, a national curriculum imposed on them by the state. Despite what some would have us believe (Russell 1993), academic freedom – especially the right to teach what one wishes in the manner one wishes – is still alive to a significant extent, even if it is being challenged (especially through the prescriptiveness of some professional bodies). Nevertheless, there are new agendas at work which would look to turn around the relationships between higher education, knowledge and society in the way suggested here. Nor is that change simply a matter of the state exerting itself, even though – in the UK, through the Enterprise in Higher Education initiative and through the quality assessment of the funding councils – we are seeing that happen.

More profoundly, we are seeing a transformation of the relationships between society and higher education. Modern society is a knowledge society but not necessarily constructed in terms of the academics' epistemologies (Stehr 1994). In all its economic and cultural institutions, society looks to higher education to supply knowledge services, but those which are addressed to its agendas. And nor is this to reify society; on the contrary. Whether postmodernity is with us or on the horizon, forms of knowing take many forms in modern society and higher education is being asked, accordingly, to widen its epistemologies. Higher education might know something about knowing but not all there is to know. Society is itself directly in the knowledge business. The universities have lost their monopoly not only over the provision of knowledge services but also over the definitions of what is to count as knowing in modern society. More operational, pragmatic and action-oriented forms of knowing are called for: academic definitions are now challenged. Consequently, higher education is having to respond to the messages coming at it anew from the wider society.

Forms of knowing

The academy has become, therefore, a site of rival versions of what it is to know the world; rival versions of competence, in effect. And the curriculum becomes the territory on which these rival versions of competence are played out.

The contest can be captured by the following list:

.knowing that	knowing how
written communication	oral communication
personal	interpersonal

internal	external
localized capacities	transferability
intellectual	physical
thought	action
problem-making	problem-solving
knowledge as process	knowledge as product
understanding	information
value-laden	'value-free'
discipline-based	issue-based
concept-based	task-based
pure	applied
proposition-based learning	experiential learning
individualized learning	group-based learning
holistic	unitized
disinterested	pragmatic
intrinsic orientation	instrumental orientation

The left-hand list of terms captures ideas central to the traditional academic understanding of higher education, while the right-hand list suggests a newer set of ideas now finding their way into higher education. The left-hand list sees student development as a means of engaging with established bodies of elaborated thought: the task for the student is one of coming to understand the world in a certain way, and being able to participate in its associated conversations. Writing, the process of engagement with others, the formation of a deep understanding, the framing of problems within disciplinary boundaries and a personal realization of the desirable attributes of disciplinary understanding: these are characteristic of the curricular components flowing from this conception of student development. In contrast, the right-hand list looks to effective action in the world. Problems are here posed by the world, and solutions are those which work pragmatically. Communication is more oral than literary and is more overtly intercommunication, but is oriented towards operations in the world. Activities have an instrumental quality, designed to bring about other ends, rather than being seen as worthwhile in themselves. Learning becomes a product rather than a process (Scott 1984).

This juxtaposition of curriculum themes and ideas should not be seen as a series of polar oppositions. These lists are not mutually exclusive. It is entirely possible for curricula to exhibit components from both lists. For example, as well as still being required to produce essays (although, in hard pressed times of rising student–staff ratios, in smaller quantities), students may well be expected to engage in activities designed to develop their powers of oral communication. Curricula may be changing so as to incorporate elements from the right-hand list rather than simply abandoning components in the left-hand list. Empirical work to determine the character of the changing scene has yet to be undertaken. Even so, what can be safely alleged is that we are at least seeing a set of changes in the higher education curriculum, with a diminution in the traditional elements focused on a deep initiation into disciplinary cultures and with a greater effort being given to action-oriented elements.

The changes are not relative but are absolute. If new elements of the kind indicated by the right-hand list are finding their way into the curriculum, elements from the left-hand list are having to be reduced, much as academics might press for a particular module on their subject to be retained and much as curricular elements tend to be added, so overloading the curriculum. Ultimately, it is realized – especially with the press of other commitments to publish, to conduct research and to generate income – that there is a limit to the additive approach and that some pruning of the traditional elements (from the left-hand list) has to be undertaken.

There is a further qualification to be made about the two lists. Their juxtaposition does not indicate that the two lists form in themselves unitary wholes. For the most part, the left-hand list does have a high degree of coherence since it reflects a form of education deriving from an agenda internal to the academy, in which human being, human identity, is largely established through a deep immersion in a disciplinary culture. Yes, there are differences between the disciplines – for example, the extent to which the conceptual apparatus is literary or numerical in character – but they are limited; the dominant set of educational aims can fall under the common description of the self-production of the academics by the academics.

The right-hand list, by contrast, reflects a mix of agendas: preparation for specific labour markets; the development of generic capacities for a changing world; the development of a higher education market, in which students are given consumer power; efficiency savings in higher education, with the university as such organizing the curriculum; and an explicit injection of the self, in self-monitoring and self-reflective capacities. These agendas are complementary to each other, reflecting an overarching instrumentalism in which higher education is governed by extra-mural considerations (of money, work, efficiency and human productivity). They are, however, different agendas, so there is no suggestion here that we are seeing a wholesale incorporation of the right-hand list of curriculum components. Different institutions and different courses within the same institution will show different patterns of movement both horizontally (in terms of a shift from left to right) and vertically (in terms of the number, range and mix of elements picked up from the right-hand list).

The new vocabulary

The changes already under way are evident in the new vocabulary with which we describe higher educational curricula. Terms such as skills, transferable skills, competence, outcomes, experiential learning, enterprise, capability, work-based learning, reflective practice and problem-based learning are only a selection from terms often used by practitioners to describe their educational intentions or curriculum aims. (Other terms, such as modular, unit, credit and access are also commonly used in relation to curricular systems, but that development – of the curriculum as a form of educational organization – is not immediately relevant here.)

A number of things are striking about the first list of terms, which primarily speak to educational intentions. First, that entire vocabulary – and, to repeat, it is only a selection – would have had little or no meaning a generation ago. The speed with which we change our understanding of higher education may be surprising. The key point, however, is that a change of this kind is not just happenchance. It is explicable; and the explanation lies in the changing set of relationships between knowledge, higher education and society with which we started our explorations. Some of the contemporary terms – such as enterprise and capability – indeed reflect national initiatives, which, in turn, indicate the way in which the wider society is now taking a close interest in the 'secret garden' of the curriculum. Through these changing relationships, actors in higher education come to understand themselves, their professional role and their pedagogical responsibilities differently. The external agendas of the wider society are, to a significant degree, internalized. Higher education comes to be different; but, more importantly, its self-understanding is different.

Second, the agendas represented by the new vocabulary are mixed, to reiterate an earlier point. But they also contain underlying dominant themes of economic competitiveness, of work effectiveness and (in the notion of transferability) of continuing self-reconstruction on the part of employees. A summary shorthand of this set of ideas is that not just of competence but of – as we might put it – operational competence.

Third, the curriculum transformations that the new terms point to are not just a matter of teaching methods but reflect a significant widening in multiple directions about what we expect of higher education in the modern age. There is a contest developing which is not just about educational aims but is one of control: who controls the curriculum in UK higher education? Until recently, it was the academics themselves. In some areas, the academics would have to bow to the power of an accrediting professional body but, even then, the relationship was usually one of partnership involving a mutual recognition of respective roles. Now, a range of different messages are coming at the university, both from the students themselves and from the state and the wider society, such that the monopoly power of the academics is being reduced. The producers are no longer free to determine the character of their own products. Indeed, their products are no longer their own; are no longer theirs.

The issue, therefore, arises as to where the power lies in determining the shape of the contemporary curriculum. Whose voices speak most powerfully? Are we seeing a displacement of the academic voice, such that it is being replaced wholesale by the new performative educational philosophies, or is it rather a messy process of negotiation and compromise? Or is it that the academics can speak the required new language – of transferable skills and problem-solving – but continue to interpret these notions in their own image. The result here would be one of incorporation rather than any substantial transformation of the student experience. The data are not to hand which would allow a clear view on the matter. What is surely clear is that the situation is uneven, that the power of the academic community differs across the sector, with the newer universities being much more permeable to the messages of the wider society while those in the older universities are still able to a significant degree to orient themselves around their disciplinary interests (see Boys *et al.* 1988). Across subjects, too, the picture differs, with some subjects able to remain relatively pure while others become infused with the agendas of the wider world.

More positively, what we can say is that the power of the academics to define curricula and educational outcomes according to their own values and interests is being eroded. This is not to accept Halsey's proletarianization thesis (Halsey 1992): it is not the case that the academics have lost completely the power to determine their own patterns of work. What is the case is that other voices, other interests, are now being represented in the framing of curricula. While mixed, those voices contain dominant agendas of performativity and operationalism. However, the very opening up of curricula and the processes of negotiation that are taking place are expanding – as we might term it – the curriculum space. Different and competing agendas find their place in this space. Reflection is to be found with performance; problem-making is to be found with problem-taking; knowing-in-the-world is to be found with knowing-in-an-intellectual-field; oral capability is to be found with aural capability; self-construction is to be found with a directedness towards given external goals.

The upshot of all of this is that the curriculum is not given in any sense. Certainly, space opens up for curricula representative of the dominant interests; but we do not have to leap from one form of closure (a curriculum in the interests of the academics) to another form of closure (a curriculum in which students are objectified as products fulfilling given operational requirements). Curricular space is now available for new kinds of curricula fulfilling even educational – as distinct from academic or instrumental – agendas.

The missing vocabulary

New discourses of learning and education emerge, therefore, but the price is that older discourses fade away. The price may be worth paying; the older discourses may have nothing to offer the modern world. A discourse which arose from a situation in which the academics had a monopoly over the definitions of knowing and learning, in which they had erected systems of knowledge 'for its own sake' but which in reality served their purposes very nicely, and which froze out other legitimate interests of the wider society, needed anyway to be severely questioned. Knowledge, research, disciplines, truth understood as propositional representations of the world and initiation of students into the conversation of a discipline (Peters 1966) sprang from the academics' professionalization of knowledge; a process which characteristically served the interests of that professional class. It also yielded a view of studenthood as a process of cognitive development through a deep insertion into a particular form of thought, offering a particular perspective on the world. The ideas of academic competence which that discourse represented cannot offer the basis for effective human being in the modern world.

Academic competence has to be repudiated epistemologically and sociologically. Epistemologically, the modern world is fundamentally problematic. We have become aware that formal knowledge systems contain their own debatable presuppositions, that academic definitions of knowledge are unduly truncated (focusing on propositional knowledge at the expense of pragmatic interpretations) and that knowledge in modern society has a recursive quality such that it always eludes full comprehension: the knowledge with which we come to know the world affects and even transforms the world (the physical environment as well as human institutions and practices), so that our knowing efforts must always be incomplete.

Sociologically, too, the world is epistemologically problematic. Our social epistemologies are now moving very fast, as cognitive definitions give way to more operational definitions. At the same time, postmodern society celebrates difference and local perspectives and eschews the kind of universalism that characterized Enlightenment thinking in the university (Scott 1997). Lastly, social change challenges individuals to reproduce themselves continually through their lifespan. Substantive knowledge is placed in the dock as redundant baggage; instead, what are now required are generic human capacities, capable of handling and deploying knowledge in pressing pragmatic situations.

The old has to give way: academic definitions of competence *are* inadequate to develop and sustain the kinds of human being that modern society, with all its challenges, presents. Yet, in this particular process of detraditionalization (Giddens 1994), in which an older tradition recedes and is supplanted by rival definitions of competence, the issue arises as to whether or not significant concepts of human being, knowing and interaction are not unduly being eschewed. A vocabulary containing, for example, disciplines, interdisciplinarity, understanding, critique and wisdom is slipping away. It slips away not so much through deliberate design but because terms such as these and the ideas that they represent are not part of the newly emerging dominant discourse, focused as it is on effective action, on outcomes and on pragmatic responsiveness.

It needs to be said, however, that in some extreme variants of the new discourse, some of the ideas associated with traditional conceptions of higher education *are* being deliberately and explicitly challenged. The NCVQ, for example, in developing its competency and outcome-based conception of education, marginalizes the notion of understanding. It is not simply that, in a performance-based approach to education, understanding is in itself problematic; although it is. In particular, the assessment of understanding takes on particular dimensions of awkwardness. But more significantly, it also appears to the proponents of the new version of education that the notion of understanding is redundant. We can set up programmes of education which yield demonstrable outcomes, which are rigorously assessed, without invoking a notion such as understanding. That which seems extraordinary, that education can be provided without *insisting* on the significance of understanding, without there being a sense that understanding matters crucially, becomes readily explicable when the world is seen through another paradigm. On the new paradigm, what matters is performance, achievement and outcomes in the world. Understanding is marginalized as a concept because it is marginal to the new performativity; it appears to be surplus to requirements.

The case for citing the other concepts in the vanishing vocabulary would have to be made for each one in turn; there is no one explicandum. Disciplines, for example, will fall out of the lexicon for two reasons. First, programmes of study will be built by individual students within a modular system around fields or clusters of interest; no longer will a disciplinary interest – the interest of the academics as monopoly providers – offer the basis of a governing set of principles. Second, and more profoundly, disciplines will recede from definitions of higher education as more pragmatic and operational definitions of knowledge and knowing come to the fore. The proliferating suffix 'studies' – as in policy studies, transport studies, tourism studies, business studies – is indicative of the way in which knowledge activities are taking their bearings from problems and processes in the world rather than formal bodies of disciplinary knowledge.

One response might be that disciplines might be losing their power as epistemological bases but that they are being supplemented by interdisciplinarity. But this is an incoherent response. If disciplines are losing their power, the chance of there being any serious attempt at interdisciplinarity – which was always a forlorn hope – has to be even slimmer. The rejoinder may come: but what of media studies, women's studies and cultural studies? Are these not interdisciplinary in character? At one level, the answer is that they may be. It is not being suggested that, suddenly, we have seen disciplines entirely disappear. But the examples cited in fact make the particular case being made here: that knowing efforts take their bearings from agendas, activities and processes in the world itself, alongside if not actually supplanting those of the disciplines as such.

As the academy and its epistemological activities become ever more inserted into the world, so in turn notions of critique and wisdom fall out of the university's self-understanding. Critique points to the setting up of alternative frameworks of understanding, and of interrogating the topic or situation in new ways, which both critique the existing modes of thought and offer new possibilities for understanding, action and interaction. Correspondingly, wisdom implies access to alternative ways of understanding the world, of going beyond the conventional. Both critique and wisdom are *both* judgemental and imaginary: critique is the more imaginary, calling up whole new ways or rival frameworks of understanding the world; wisdom couples to judgement an insight into a specific situation, offering a progressive way forward not immediately available through the given understandings. It is hardly surprising if both terms seem out-of-kilter with the emerging dominant ways of thinking of higher education, for both terms – if they are to have application – depend on there being an institutional space in which alternative frameworks for understanding the world are likely to be generated.

A danger, therefore, with the current lurch in the direction of operational competence is that our conception of higher education will be narrowed, with students just being expected to take on the capacities for immediate responsiveness. The pilot may, or may not, be able to bring the oil tanker safely into the port, but where are the larger questions being asked about the likely ecological effects of any accident, about the transport policies which encourage the use of the motor car, not to mention whether other technological 'solutions' might be found which would render unnecessary the manoeuvring of a large tanker into a narrow inlet?

Two rival versions of competence

What we are currently seeing in UK higher education is not simply the arrival of a competency-based model of education: that is a totally inadequate way of understanding the situation. It is inadequate in two ways.

First, the competency-based model does not itself just arrive in and by itself. The so-called competency-based model is but one set of definitions of competence, in which competence is construed in operational terms. This conception of competence has to be understood as a response to contemporary understandings and practices in higher education. It is not that the academic world has never possessed a sense of the desirability of developing competent graduates, but rather that the academic world has understood competence in different terms; in short, in *its* terms. The academic world's conception of competence has hinged on a deep initiation into forms of thought that it found worthwhile: the competence lay in the student being able to show that she had not only mastered a body of propositional knowledge but also intuited the form of life which the form of understanding embodied. Becoming a *competent* member of that discourse community was precisely the hope and expectation. Competence was understood here not only at the level of understanding the particular perspective on the world that the form of experience offered (what made physics different from chemistry; what made sociology different from philosophy; what made economics different from history), but also *operationally*: the graduate had to demonstrate a capacity to make the permitted communicative moves, to handle the key concepts in the acceptable fashion, to deploy the tacit

Table 2.1   Two rival versions of competence

		Operational competence	Academic competence
1	Epistemology	Know how	Know that
2	Situations	Defined pragmatically	Defined by intellectual field
3	Focus	Outcomes	Propositions
4	Transferability	Meta-operations	Meta-cognition
5	Learning	Experiential	Propositional
6	Communication	Strategic	Disciplinary
7	Evaluation	Economic	Truthfulness
8	Value orientation	Economic survival	Disciplinary strength
9	Boundary conditions	Organizational norms	Norms of intellectual field
10	Critique	For better practical effectiveness	For better cognitive understanding

methods associated with the discipline and to articulate ideas within the local conventions.

So an intellectual and a methodological competence was to be found in the academics' definitions of education; unfortunately, it is not the competence now sought from the voices extra-mural to the academy. This academic competence, accordingly, is not real competence, is not now seen as competence. The new definition of competence displays its operationalism explicitly, and rules offside the older definition as entirely inappropriate for the modern age. We have, then, not one version of competence but two rival versions of competence. In summary form, those two versions of competence have the structure shown in Table 2.1.

I said earlier that the sense that we are now seeing the arrival of a competency-based model of higher education is an inadequate construal of the situation for two reasons. The first has just been set out: we have had a competency-based model of higher education for some time; it is just that the existing definition of competence – the academics' definition of competence – is not the new definition of competence. The new definition of competence attempts to capture the discourse of competence by pretending that it alone holds the key to the door of competence; that its definition of competence is the true definition. However, this is but a nice example of discursive hegemony in action.

The second reason – for expressing caution against seeing this contest simply as one of rival versions of an educational approach – emerges in Table 2.1. What is at stake is not just educational approach or even educational 'philosophy'. It is a much larger matter. What this contest amounts to is, to reiterate a point, a shift in our social epistemologies. Essentially, these two definitions of competence amount to a major change in the way in which we come to know the world. What counts as knowledge is not a matter to be left to the philosophers or educationalists but is a set of understandings in society. There will be different and competing ideas in society – as Table 2.1 indicates – but that there is a contest over ways of knowing suggests that some definitions might be more powerful and more influential than others.

I contend that we are currently witnessing a shift in our sense of what it is to know the world of a fundamental kind. In essence, the shift is a move away from contemplative versions of knowledge to pragmatic and operational versions of knowledge. To deploy Gilbert Ryle's phrases, we are seeing a move in our ways of knowing the world from knowing that to knowing how (Ryle 1949). (Ryle, we should note, did not put it this way, and the sudden contemporary usage of his terminology does little justice to Ryle's arguments.) Academics have attempted, through a range of methodologies and conceptual frameworks, to distance themselves from the world and to come to know the world as it is. Both the correspondence and the coherence views of truth contain this sense of truth as being independent of the world. Now, that sense of knowing is challenged. In its place, we are being urged to adopt more pragmatic definitions of knowing the world. One can come to know the world in legitimate ways through acting in it and on it. Notions of the reflective practitioner, action learning and tacit knowledge all speak immediately to this new interest. Other notions, such as problem-solving and trial-and-error, also come to have pragmatic rather than contemplative interpretations. What counts as knowledge is what is seen to have instrumental effects of appropriate kinds in the world, preferably effects which are likely to promote a society of continuing change and which are likely to aid economic competitiveness.

Operational competence in the curriculum, therefore, has to be seen against this background of a shift in our social epistemologies, our general sense in society as to what is to count as knowledge. This shift picks up a point I made at the start of this chapter, that our academies are no longer able to define for themselves what is to count as knowing (and, therefore, what is to count as learning) but are having to respond to wider societal and even global shifts. The university is fast becoming an institution of society rather than an institution in society. What now is coming to count in our education of our students is the question: 'what can she do?' (Lyotard 1984). 'What does she know?' is much less in evidence. But again, to make the point, this is not just a shift from knowledge to skills; it is a transformation in how we understand what it is to know the world. Knowledge for effectiveness supplants knowledge for understanding.

A third possibility

If, as I contend, there are basically two rival versions of higher education squaring up to each other, how might we move forward? We have to be clear that there can be no cobbling together of these versions of competence – academic and operational – so as to provide a neat compromise solution. It cannot be a matter of a judicious mix of the two sets of ideas so that the student receives a balanced curriculum (see Goodlad 1995); and for two reasons. First, as we have seen, these are *rival* versions of human being. Being rival versions does not, admittedly, make them entirely contra-dictory, one with another. But they are marked by schisms, such as the centrality of understanding in one version and its neglect in the other, in the criteria for truth (coherence and correspondence on the one hand and pragmatism on the other) and their fundamental purposes (disciplinary engagement and economic competitiveness). These are different ways of looking at the world. Simply compiling a curriculum by pulling elements from the two versions of competence is likely only to end in a mish-mash, a thoroughly incoherent experience for the student and a falling short of any stable set of aims.

The other reason why no compromise solution is readily available is even more serious. It is that *neither* version of competence remotely comes close to meeting the requirements of the modern age. And if that is so, a curric-ulum which brings elements together from those two sets of views is itself bound to fall well short of the needs of our age. The main challenge of the modern world arises out of change, but it is not change itself. Change is itself a challenge; hence the loose talk of transferable skills and adaptability. But the main challenge is more far-reaching. It is that the modern world is unknowable. Whether or not we can sensibly talk of 'a runaway world' (Giddens 1994) is a moot point. What is clear is that the Western university, which has been founded on a knowledge project, on a sense that the world is knowable, has – in a world which is unknowable – to reconsider its role and, thereby, the education it offers to its students.

There are several senses in which the world is unknowable and they can only be stated here. First, in a literate society, knowledge is socially reflex-ive. At one level, this imparts control and underwrites the knowledge project. But, because people can and do modify their understanding of their world, of themselves and of their practices within it in ways which are themselves unpredictable, there arises an epistemological instability. The world is al-ways moving on in advance of our efforts to understand it. Second, we have become sceptical of the hegemonic claims of any particular framework and, indeed, of professional expertise. We have a sense that all kinds of explana-tions and accounts of the world are not just possible but are legitimate. But some of these frameworks may be incommensurable between themselves and there is no way to legislate between them. Third, we know now that there are few, if any, secure knowledge claims; even the hard sciences pro-duce few incontestable claims, while the technologies which are linked to those sciences are forever coming unstuck. Fourth, the knowledge project of the Western university has been tied to the prospect of gaining control over the world. But the world is now wreaking its vengeance through the ecological crisis and many other manifestations of the limits of control. In turn, more naturalistic frameworks of understanding and engagement are arising, in relation to our interactions both with the world and with each other. But these frameworks are both contested and inherently lacking in absolute claims on the world. Lastly, the category of the postmodern urges on us caution in believing that there are any absolute criteria or principles which might govern our approaches to knowing the world and understanding each other. There are no absolute rules of right reason. It is not just that we cannot easily judge between rival frameworks; in a world which expresses an 'incredulity towards metanarratives' (Lyotard 1984), we have no non-controversial rules for judging in the first place (see Myerson 1994).

If the world is unknowable, if it is subject to ceaseless change, if we have multiple but incommensurable frameworks being offered to us, if there are no reliable experts, if we cannot even be sure about the rules for reasoning and interaction, what then becomes of the university and its higher education? Clearly, versions of competence – academic or operational – make no sense. In this world, we do not know what it is to be competent; it is not at all clear that competence has any useful meaning. What then?

If we are to produce a higher education fit for the new century with all its challenges, uncertainties, change – in short, its unknowable character – we need a quite different way of looking at the problem. The two rival versions of competence both have to be jettisoned as entirely inadequate for the modern age. What is required is a higher education which is likely to foster the personal, cognitive and social capacities that the modern age requires. Conceptions of higher education based on competence of whatever kind cannot do this. In a world of change, radical uncertainty and unfathomable complexity, human capacities are required which are able to challenge any existing notion of competence. A higher education has, therefore, to promote the highest forms of human learning likely to develop the qualities required if people and society are to prosper in such an age.

The notion of competence is hopelessly wrong for this reason. Competence implies a known situation and well understood attributes – whether of skills and knowledge – which are appropriate to effectiveness in that situation. In an age of radical change and uncertainty, situations are not given and the appropriate knowledge and skills are contested. Instead, what are required are meta-abilities which enable people, both individually and collectively, to handle change, openness, conflict and uncertainty. There are two ingredients here: reflexivity and the power to go on reconstituting oneself – with others – through one's lifespan. The self is not given; and nor are our frameworks for comprehending the world. These have to go on being subject to continual interrogation. We live effectively and prosperously in a world of change by changing ourselves so that we in turn can contribute actively to changes in the most general sense. I call this (to adopt some of the terminology of Jurgen Habermas 1991) life-world becoming. We create ourselves, we become ourselves, perpetually and, in so doing, assist in the recreation of the world around us. The way in which such a conception of education maps on to the two rival versions of competence is shown in Table 2.2.

The notion of the 'life-world' picks up non-instrumental aspects of life but it is not just pointing to personal and existential conditions of life. The

Table 2.2 Beyond competence

		Operational competence	Academic competence	Life-world becoming
1	Epistemology	Know how	Know that	Reflective knowing
2	Situations	Defined pragmatically	Defined by intellectual field	Open definition (with use of multiple approaches)
3	Focus	Outcomes	Propositions	Dialogue and argument as such
4	Transferability	Meta-operations	Meta-cognition	Meta-critique
5	Learning	Experiential	Propositional	Meta-learning
6	Communication	Strategic	Disciplinary	Dialogical
7	Evaluation	Economic	Truthfulness	Consensus
8	Value orientation	Economic survival	Relative strength of discipline	The 'common good' (defined consensually)
9	Boundary conditions	Organizational norms	Norms of intellectual field	Practicalities of discourse
10	Critique	For better practical effectiveness	For better cognitive understanding	For better practical understanding

life-world also incorporates a sense of traditions, of community, and of solidarity. The notion of becoming, however, indicates that those dimensions of life have, in the modern world, to be subject to continual interrogation and made to live effectively in the modern world by undergoing change, change brought about by our own mutually reflective practices. (This, by the way, is just one reason why the notion of 'the reflective practitioner' is also inadequate, since it offers no account of the mutuality of professional life and the need for professionals collectively to engage in a process of professional reconstruction.)

The key elements of the third column, 'life-world becoming', are those of reflexivity, dialogue, meta-critique and practical understanding. This conception, therefore, looks neither to traditions of cognition (even if those traditions are malleable) nor to given situations requiring identified skills (even if those situations are complex and require some adroitness in their handling). Instead, this conception recognizes a world in which all bets are off, so to speak, and where the only means of effective survival is for us collectively to go on reviewing the world we are in and refashioning it and ourselves in the process. The refashioning, of course, will include considerations of what it is to know and to live effectively in the world. No consensus is assumed on any matter; but, for meaningful dialogue to take place, there would need to be some agreement on elementary rules of rational engagement. Beyond that, the worlds we live in – cognitively, socially, culturally, technologically, existentially – would result from our collective engagements with each other and in the context of our collective understandings of the world. A higher education for the modern age would be one which fostered such human – cognitive, personal and interpersonal – capacities. Unless we redesign and reconceive of higher education, as we move into a new century, in these ambitious ways, it will fall short of the challenges ahead of us all in living effectively in a world of unknown change and challenge.

Conclusion

Higher education is a social institution of extreme longevity. A product of medieval Europe, it has become a truly global institution and has lasted nearly a thousand years. It has done so because it has continued to adapt; and, indeed, the pace of adaptation has accelerated, especially over the last half of the present century. The future, therefore, perhaps seems assured. There is no real difficulty: the university will easily adapt to the require-ments of the new age. The emerging debate over the curriculum and the language of competence is only – so it might be argued – a symptom of the contemporary phase of adaptation. Soon, the dust will settle and we will be clear about the way forward.

I have tried to show that such sanguinity is misplaced. The available ways of construing higher education are utterly inadequate to the modern age. The university has derived its legitimacy from a project built around knowl-edge, around knowing the world. But the modern world is unknowable – not only epistemologically, socially and culturally, but in terms of our personal identities. Against this background, the academics' reliance on knowledge competences has to be called into question, but the so-called competency movement is equally culpable, for it also rests on assumptions that the world is knowable (and the task is one of identifying and delivering the required competences).

We need, therefore, to do nothing short of jettisoning the whole way we have construed higher education for one thousand years and, instead, work out a new conception of education which starts from the understanding that the world is unknowable in any serious sense. We have to develop a form of *higher* education which allows for the continuing examination and construction of self, society and culture, including our ways of knowing and of understanding the world about us and of acting in it. This is an educa-tion for life-world becoming and it is legitimately termed *higher* education since it calls for meta-capacities – of knowing, of self-understanding and of communication. In short, we have to abandon the conception of both a higher education in society and a higher education of society, and develop, instead, a higher education for society.

An education for an unknowable world – unknowable partly because we are reconstructing ourselves and our world – requires literally a revolution in the practices we term higher education. Unless we can achieve this, however, we are destined to live in a runaway world.

References

Boys, C. *et al.* (1988) *Higher Education and the Preparation for Work.* London, Jessica Kingsley.

Fuller, T. (ed.) (1989) *The Voice of Liberal Learning: Michael Oakeshott on Education.* London, Yale.

Gellner, E. (1991) *Plough, Sword and Book: the Structure of Human History.* London, Paladin.

Gibbons, M. *et al.* (1994) *The New Production of Knowledge: the Dynamics of Science and Research in Contemporary Societies.* London, Sage.

Giddens, A. (1994) *Beyond Left and Right.* Cambridge, Polity Press.

Goodlad, S. (1995) *The Quest for Quality: Sixteen Forms of Heresy in Higher Education.* Buckingham, Open University Press/SRHE.

Habermas, J. (1991) *The Theory of Communicative Action, Vol. 1.* Cambridge, Polity Press.

Hague, D. (1991) *Beyond Universities: a New Republic of the Intellect.* London, IEA.

Halsey, A. H. (1992) *The Decline of Donnish Dominion.* Oxford, Oxford University Press.

Hyland, T. (1994) *Competence, Education and NVQs: Dissenting Perspectives.* London, Cassell.

Lyotard, J.-F. (1984) *The Postmodern Condition: a Report on Knowledge.* Manchester, Manchester University Press.

Myerson, G. (1994) *Rhetoric, Reason and Society.* London, Sage.

Peters, R. S. (1966) *Ethics and Education.* London, George Allen and Unwin.

Russell, C. (1993) *Academic Freedom.* London, Routledge.

Ryle, G. (1949) *The Concept of Mind.* Harmondsworth, Penguin.

Scott, P. (1997) The crisis of knowledge and the massification of higher education, in R. Barnett and A. Griffin (eds) *Higher Education: Knowledge Crisis.* London, Cassell.

Scott, P. (1984) *The Crisis of the University.* Beckenham, Croom Helm.

Stehr, N. (1994) *Knowledge Societies.* London, Sage.

3

Enhancing Quality

Robin Middlehurst

Introduction

'Quality' was the buzz word for the 1980s and 'standards' appear to be the preoccupation of the 1990s. Both are contested concepts (Barnett 1992), since they are almost invariably linked to different sets of values and interests, and may be interpreted differently in different contexts. What is meant by these terms, particularly in the balance of emphasis that is placed on 'quality assurance' as an aspect of accountability or 'quality enhancement' as a feature of institutional or departmental development, has important consequences for daily academic practice.

In this chapter, I shall briefly explore the context and concepts of quality and standards before discussing approaches to quality assurance and enhancement at local and national levels. A dominant theme that emerges from this analysis is the emphasis placed on accountability, in contrast to, and perhaps at the expense of, improvement and development. The consequences of this emphasis are examined with reference to quality management and improvement approaches outside higher education. The chapter ends with a number of suggestions about ways in which to concentrate more effectively on quality enhancement in higher education.

Concepts and context of quality and standards

As studies of quality in higher education and elsewhere have shown (Collard 1993; Williams *et al.* 1993; Green 1994), quality is understood to mean different things. At one end of a spectrum, there is a sense in which quality can mean whatever individuals or groups take it to mean according to their own tastes and needs. Notions of quality as fitness for purpose, where purpose is defined (typically) in terms of customer requirements, fall into this category. At the other end of the spectrum, quality can be interpreted as the attainment of a level of excellence that is defined, tacitly or explicitly,

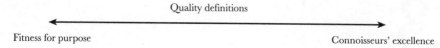

Figure 3.1 Spectrum of 'quality' definitions.

by those who are expected to understand and recognize such excellence, the 'connoisseurs' (see Figure 3.1).

These examples suggest that whenever judgements of the utility and value of a product or process are called for, 'quality' becomes entangled with different expectations and requirements. Much of the debate has focused on quality both as a process and as an outcome. Debate in all sectors has therefore involved attempts to determine: (1) different process and, particularly, output requirements; (2) a process that can transform inputs to desired outputs reliably, consistently and in forms which are tailored to different needs; (3) a process and outcomes which are recognized as satisfactory to clients, external interests and providers; and (4) a process and outcomes that are distinctive and reputable. A consistent backdrop to the determination of quality in all organizations is the economic imperative of competition for markets and resources and the inexorable march of technology.

Higher education, because of the wide and diverse nature of its business, provides an interesting microcosm of the quality universe and a clear illustration of the issues involved in determining what quality is and how it can be achieved, assured and improved. To take each of the above four points in turn:

1. In different institutions, departments or programme areas, debate continues as to whether the chief focus of activity should be on high-quality research output or high-quality graduates, or both; and if both, what teaching, learning and research processes are most appropriate to achieving the agreed objectives at a time of resource constraint, international competition and technological development. Internal debate is mirrored by debate on similar topics by interest groups, such as employers, professional bodies or government departments. The conclusions of each group are unlikely to be the same.
2. The forms of internal quality management are very diverse in higher education. Some institutions and many academic units have yet to develop clearly articulated approaches to quality management; indeed, in some cases, management itself has yet to become embedded as a valued feature of higher education. Variations in consistency and reliability of the services offered are still to be found within and between institutions, and, with larger and more diverse numbers of students, the balance between consistency and fairness to all, and tailored provision for individuals and groups according to their needs, is still to be worked out.
3. At the heart of the present discussions about appropriate forms of

national quality assurance in the UK (which are designed to integrate quality audit and quality assessment; internal quality control, evaluation and development; and accreditation by professional bodies) lie debates about autonomy, responsibility and accountability in the provision of higher education. And beneath this, there are still more fundamental concerns related to the nature and standards of graduate education for the twenty-first century, which reflect different notions of what higher education is for, what it should be aiming to achieve, whose priorities should take precedence and who should pay for its services and products. The debate continues.

4. Ultimately, a goal for any organization must be to have its name, products or services become synonymous with 'quality'. For this to happen, quality and continuous improvement, as the quality gurus argue (Bendell 1991), must become a way of life in the organization and the organization must also seek continually to differentiate itself from its competitors. There are many examples in higher education where institutions, individuals or academic units are aiming at this goal, but there is also a worrying degree of conformity despite the rhetoric of diversity. Ironically, perhaps, conformity and compliance seem to be encouraged by external measurements of quality in research and teaching, associated with current funding regimes.

Until recently, public debate in higher education has focused on 'quality' and the means of assuring it, both within institutions, for the purposes of internal management, and externally, for public accountability to taxpayer and student. However, as many other sectors have learnt, it is difficult to discuss, and particularly to try to measure, quality without mentioning standards, since judgements of quality tend to be made in relation to explicit or implicit standards. These standards represent yardsticks against which to judge quality in relation to particular dimensions, such as overall performance, utility, safety or aesthetic value.

To take the spectrum in Figure 3.1, the standards reflected in a 'fitness for purpose' definition of quality would be those measures which were defined by individual providers (or customers) of higher education. These standards could vary quite considerably. Contrastingly, the standards of connoisseurship, represented as 'excellent quality', are measures of value which are commonly accepted among a group and may therefore have wider currency. In practice in higher education, both notions of standards (and therefore quality) appear to operate simultaneously, which makes for a general lack of clarity and focus. For example, the public assessment of teaching quality is formally made against the standard set (however implicitly) by a subject provider – a 'fitness for purpose' definition. Judgements of academic standards, on the other hand, which are made, for example, by external examiners within a subject area, are made on the basis of 'connoisseurship', i.e. the extent to which the standards of academic performance in one programme are broadly comparable with others, as measured

Explanation of objectives
Incremental improvement
Alternative approaches
Transformation

Figure 3.2   Levels of quality enhancement.

against a notion of 'academic excellence' which is tacitly shared among a group. Current debates about standards (Higher Education Quality Council 1995) illustrate the difficulties of trying to use both notions simultaneously, particularly since many of these standards are tacit and implicit. It is partly for this reason and partly for reasons of transparency and accountability that there are calls for greater explicitness in relation to standards; as Peter Williams, Director of Quality Assurance at the Higher Education Quality Council has said, a connoisseur's approach to quality and standards is under pressure from a new, 'forensic' approach.

Quality assurance, quality enhancement and standards as aspects of quality management

Quality assurance and quality enhancement are not the same, although they are clearly connected. Both depend on an appreciation of the context and meaning of quality for an individual, group or unit and both should be built upon a specification of (educational) purposes, aims and objectives as well as standards which can guide judgements of performance. Beyond this, however, the two are dissimilar, since quality assurance is concerned with establishing that objectives are being achieved consistently and reliably, while quality enhancement is concerned with improving on or changing the original objectives, aims or purposes.

By examining different ways in which academic units and whole institutions are approaching quality enhancement, as in Figure 3.2, it is possible to identify an assurance and enhancement framework linked to different stages of development in quality management.

At a basic level, enhancement of quality involves examining what one is doing and, as a consequence, making explicit aims, objectives and outcomes. This review and 'explanatory' stage may of itself enhance practice by exposing anomalies or gaps in current activities. At the next level, enhancement may involve making incremental changes so that teaching is more efficient or research more productive, while maintaining the current direction of each. At a third level, quality enhancement will involve doing things in new ways; for example, by developing a distance-learning form of

Figure 3.3 Stages of development in approaches to quality.

a traditional undergraduate programme or a thematic rather than individually driven approach to research. The most radical forms of quality enhancement are those which involve transformational changes that call for a complete re-examination, re-conceptualization and re-direction of existing practice, perhaps related to the introduction of a modular degree scheme or to the establishment of a regional higher education 'federation'. Some institutions and units are engaged in transformations of these kinds and many more will need to be as the pressures on teaching resources rise, the competition for research contracts and grants accelerates or technological developments force radical thinking and action.

These approaches to quality enhancement can be put within a more general and widely known framework representing stages of quality management (see Figure 3.3).

Within this framework, an initial stage will involve specifying what one is trying to achieve in relation to a set of purposes and goals. In order to measure levels of attainment, standards will also need to be part of this specification. Typically, the next stage of development will involve quality control, i.e. procedures to check whether objectives have been achieved at the desired performance level. Beyond this level lies quality assurance, which involves establishing that there are systems and procedures in place to ensure that objectives are met consistently and reliably, and that they are periodically reviewed. Quality enhancement can be conceived as a subsequent (and consequent) stage of each of these dimensions. For example, quality enhancement should follow from quality control by correcting errors or plugging gaps in the achievement of objectives. Quality enhancement should also flow out from quality assurance by investigating and correcting failures or lacunae in systems and procedures and by spreading good practice identified in the review of one area of activity by disseminating this to other areas. In these forms, quality enhancement is part of a feedback loop which, if recognized, noted and acted upon, should lead to incremental improvements in practice.

However, approaches to quality enhancement of this kind are essentially reactive and driven by the internal workings of a process; for example, a programme of teaching or the operations of a department. A distinctive

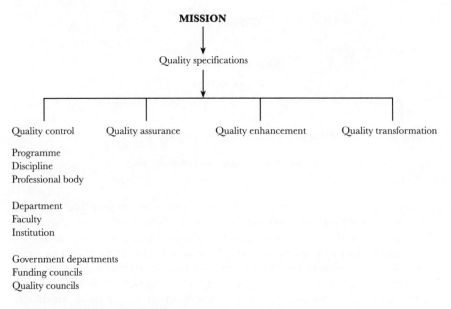

Figure 3.4 Matrix of approaches to quality in higher education.

feature of quality enhancement at the next stage of development is the inclusion of external feedback (for example, feedback from external stake-holders or data from benchmarking against other institutions) and external intelligence as a normal part of continuously re-evaluating objectives against stakeholder/client requirements, national or international competition, community needs etc. At this level, quality enhancement does not have to be tied to the workings of internal processes but can operate proactively. And finally, at a level beyond this, quality enhancement becomes quality transformation, as described earlier. In this case, not only are all sources of feedback and learning utilized to improve and develop current practice, but the objectives and assumptions underlying existing practice are con-stantly challenged so as to create new ways of doing things. Single-loop learning has changed into double-loop learning (Morgan 1986).

   If one takes this discussion a stage further, it is possible to map these stages of development on to the approaches to quality that have been adopted at different levels of an institution, at national level or in different disciplin-ary/professional areas. A matrix then emerges as in Figure 3.4.

   The establishment of standards is integral to notions of quality at all stages and in all aspects of quality management. These standards may be readily quantifiable in some areas (for example, numbers of days taken to return assessed work to students) and in others may be less readily quan-tified (for example, the nature of the intellectual development achieved by a student between years one and two of a programme of study). Whether they can be quantified precisely or not, they represent important targets to aim at as well as necessary yardsticks for measuring success, for identifying progress and for making comparisons.

Figure 3.5 is a representation of approaches to quality and standards at national level in higher education. This illustrates the quality management spectrum in relation to dimensions of assurance/accountability and enhancement/transformation. The focus of these activities at national level is on system-wide and institutional development, in contrast to quality management at local level, which is likely to focus upon development at group and individual levels as well as at institutional level. Figure 3.5 also shows how standards fit into the picture and what activities are undertaken (or could be undertaken) under the various headings.

Improvement and accountability

Figure 3.5 illustrates how the purposes of enhancement and transformation can be addressed and how accountability stands in relationship to these purposes. While this figure places a much larger emphasis on enhancement and change, such an emphasis is not obvious in practice. Most of the national (and local) effort that is expended on quality is focused on the accountability/assurance end of the spectrum rather than the improvement/change end – although it is often argued that if accountability is demonstrated, improvement will follow. There are a number of flaws in this argument and a number of consequences which flow from an overemphasis on accountability at the expense of improvement.

The first flaw is that there is a necessary relationship between accountability and improvement; this is not the case, since they may each serve a range of different purposes and interests, some of which are likely to be in conflict with each other. (Table 3.1 offers some contrasts between improvement and accountability.) For example, there are at least six major external groups which may have a legitimate claim on accountability from higher education for the services it offers: government (as sponsors and funders of large parts of higher education); employers (as recruiters of graduates and as customers seeking professional updating for their employees); industry and commerce (as consumers of and contributors to research and consultancy); communities (seeking cultural, social and economic regeneration); students (as seekers and beneficiaries of a higher education experience); the professions (as regulators and developers of professional practice). However, internal groups are no less important. Academics are likely to have a view of accountability linked to peer recognition and disciplinary/professional development. Institutions will have an interest linked to survival and renewal, and other groups of staff are likely to have interests related to fair employment and to personal or professional advancement. For the most part, the present focus of accountability is on satisfying external rather than internal interests.

If one examines what these groups seek in the way of accountability,

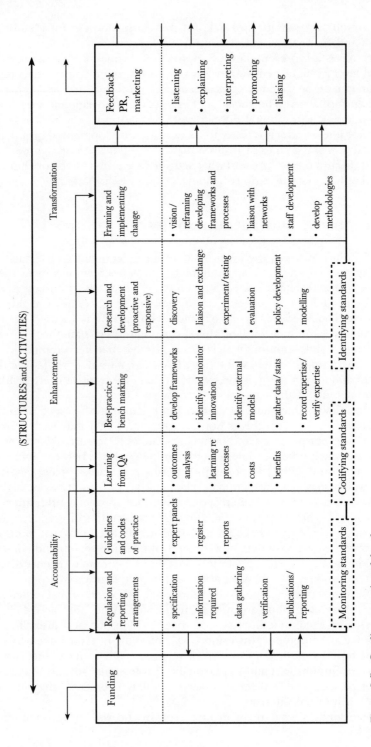

Figure 3.5 Quality at national level.

Table 3.1 Contrasts between approaches to improvement and accountability

Improvement	*Accountability*
Internal interests	External interests
Evaluation	Inspection
Intrinsic motivation	Extrinsic motivation
Empowerment	Control
Learning	Information

the range of differences between interests are obvious; for example, cost-effectiveness, value for (taxpayers') money, social and economic returns on investment, qualifications and new learning (acquired efficiently and effectively), market share, responsiveness to technological developments, professional satisfaction and achievement, personal or institutional survival. Similar differences in perspective occur when one considers the purposes and focus of improvements. Students may wish to see improved access to library materials or computer terminals; employers may wish to see curricular developments; funding councils may wish to see improved managerial efficiency; academics may wish to see improvements in the time and other resources available for research. All of these reflect differences in values and priorities, and once again, external interests tend to dominate.

A second flaw is based on the assumption that the motivations which drive individuals and institutions to be 'accountable' in response to the interests of external stakeholders are the same motivations as those which drive improvements in practice. The motivations involved are not the same. Accountability as currently practised relies largely on extrinsic motivation. For example, providers of higher education must first acknowledge the legitimate interests of those groups who seek accountability from them. Providers then need to understand and accept the nature of what is being sought (for example, an up-to-date curriculum, fitting students for employment; or an institution that can verify its claims in offering higher education at a standard comparable to other such institutions). Providers will also need to be clear about the terms in which accountability is to be rendered. These terms and conditions for accountability are not necessarily those that a provider of higher education would set for itself.

Any gains from the process, as well as ownership of the process, lie primarily with external interests. In addition, it is assumed that the extrinsic motivator of competition will operate through the lever of accountability to promote improvement. At the lowest level, institutions will seek to avoid public embarrassment and loss of reputation by rendering an account of themselves in line with external expectations, since quality reports are made public. At higher levels, institutions will compete to out-perform each other to achieve maximum numbers of 'high quality' judgements – at least for the duration of the competitive period.

In sharp contrast, effective and sustained improvement tends to rely on intrinsic motivation, often linked to notions of professionalism. Benefits and ownership of improvements also need to be linked to internally driven interests, since improvement requires an acknowledgement of a need to improve, an understanding of the appropriate focus for improvement, a knowledge of how to achieve the objectives of improvement and an appreciation of and desire for the benefits which will accrue from the effort. In other words, improvement relies upon individuals and groups engaging with the desired objectives and a commitment to their achievement. Unless improvement is driven by a large measure of intrinsic motivation, the best that can be hoped for is compliance with external requirements. Compliance may pass for improvement in the short term, but as soon as the need for display is over, old habits are likely to re-emerge.

A third issue involves the concept of quality enhancement that is linked with accountability. In many cases, quality enhancement is only associated with the outcomes of quality control, assurance or external evaluation. In practice, this may mean that there is a greater concentration on incremental and largely reactive improvements in practice rather than on more radical reassessment and redirecting of practice. At a time when higher education needs to be looking outwards in order to act on the basis of external intelligence, and when scarce resources, technological developments and market pressures require urgent and often radical action from institutions and academic units, incrementalism is an insufficient and possibly dangerous response.

It is of course necessary to be able to claim, with a large degree of certainty and confidence, that one is delivering a high-quality education to students or a high-quality research programme to sponsors. It is also necessary for students and sponsors to feel secure in trusting such claims, in relation to both present and future educational opportunities and research contracts. The 'forensic' culture requires evidence over assertion to support claims for quality and standards, and this means that quality assurance and accountability are important features in institutional quality management.

However, over-concentration on 'rendering an account' to external audiences can take time and resources away from delivering high-quality education or research, or finding out the real needs of students and sponsors and developing new approaches to satisfying their requirements in cost-effective ways. Undertaking change, whether it arises from quality control/assurance evidence or from other sources, will also require resources as well as the will and power to make it happen. As studies of leadership and the management of change suggest (Kanter 1985; Kotter 1990; Middlehurst 1993), key ingredients for high performance and successful and lasting change are ownership of the process, commitment and effort towards achieving the desired goals, resources devoted to the process and trust in the professionals involved.

Within higher education, there is a need to focus on approaches to quality management which are more holistic and which give much greater

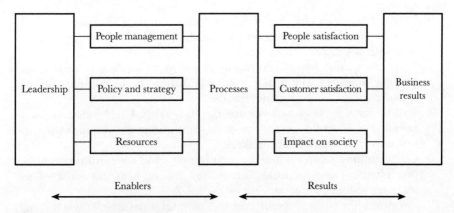

Figure 3.6 European Quality Award.

attention to forms of quality enhancement that are proactive and outward-looking and that actively rely upon professional responsibility and commitment. Some models which are attracting attention include the Investors in People standard and the European Quality Award. Both approaches focus much more closely on effective leadership and professional development, which tend to be missing dimensions in debates on quality in higher education (Middlehurst and Gordon 1995). These models are worth exploring; the latter is presented in Figure 3.6.

Ways forward

There is much that needs to be done to advance the quality enhancement agenda in higher education. The following ideas are put forward as a starting point for action at national and local levels.

1. Integrate effort by clarifying and differentiating the roles of different enhancement agents within institutions and at national level in order to avoid unnecessary duplication or conflict.
2. Target resources towards making accessible the widest range of effective teaching, learning, student support and assessment methods through peer-group networks.
3. Benchmark good practice and celebrate success through national guidance (locally interpreted), supported by databases, networks, conferences, publications, awards and performance indicators.
4. Achieve parity of esteem between teaching and research so that students' educational opportunities are maximized and staff expertise is recognized and rewarded.
5. Invest in research and development by building an effective educational 'R & D' base which can underpin higher education practice from organizational to individual levels.

6. Learn from others by identifying and disseminating ideas and practice from outside higher education and building open communication channels with all stakeholders.
7. Focus on quality by concentrating attention and giving priority to improving activities that make a critical difference to students' educational experience and achievements.
8. Build a new professional culture through critical self-evaluation, support for staff and a commitment to continuous development for the institution and individuals alike.
9. Clarify minimum accountability requirements and concentrate resources on delivering the essentials, while also making maximum use of the learning gained from the process.
10. Pay attention to leadership and the management of change through professional responsibility and development in order to achieve high quality/high standards in higher education.

References

Barnett, R. (1992) *Improving Higher Education: Total Quality Care.* Buckingham, Open University Press/SRHE.

Bendell, T. (1991) *The Quality Gurus.* London, Department of Trade and Industry.

Collard, R. (1993) *Total Quality: Success through People,* 2nd edn. Wimbledon, Institute of Personnel Management.

Green, D. (ed.) (1994) *What Is Quality in Higher Education?* Buckingham, Open University Press/SRHE.

Higher Education Quality Council (1995) *Graduate Standards: Interim Report.* London, HEQC.

Kanter, R. (1985) *The Change Masters.* New York, Simon & Schuster.

Kotter, J. (1990) *A Force for Change: How Leadership Differs from Management.* New York, Free Press.

Merli, G. (1993) *Eurochallenge: the TQM Approach to Capturing Global Markets.* Bedford, IFS Ltd.

Middlehurst, R. (1993) *Leading Academics.* Buckingham, Open University Press/SRHE.

Middlehurst, R. and Gordon, G. (1995) Leadership, quality and institutional effectiveness, *Higher Education Quarterly,* 49(3), 267–85.

Morgan, G. (1986) *Images of Organisation.* London, Sage.

Williams, G., Loder, C. and Fry, H. (1993) *Leverhulme Project: Quality in Higher Education.* London, Centre for Higher Education Studies, Institute of Education.

4

Towards a Lifelong Curriculum

Chris Duke

Introduction: reductionism and the impoverishment of vision

Lifelong learning and the learning society are the talk of the academic town in 1996, the European Year of Lifelong Learning. With inspired timing, a European daughter, ELLI (European Lifelong Learning Institute), has sprung from the loins of an intendedly worldwide, lifelong learning institute launched in 1994. Has lifelong learning come of age? What does it all mean for the university and higher education?

A central theme of this chapter is reductionism and the impoverishment of vision which besets much educational planning, even as the term vision climbs in favour: desirably, values and vision precede and direct the mission from which flow strategic planning and operations. A recent document considering the development of higher level National Vocational Qualifications used the word vision, but the text was widely criticized for reading more like bureaucratic tidying up. It is frequently said that the blight of British, or rather and more especially English, education and society, on which this chapter concentrates, is poverty of aspiration. Compare the recent British and European discussion papers on lifelong learning. The former was roundly criticized, among others by the generally cautious Committee of Vice Chancellors and Principals, for lacking an overall sense of vision, taking a largely instrumental view, reinforcing an obsolete 'vocational–non-vocational' divide and failing to recognize the contribution of universities (DfEE 1995; CVCP 1996). The latter, for all that it too attracted critical comment, took a far larger and wider view of society, its social concerns and its educational needs (European Commission 1995).

Post-imperial, postmodern, English society lacks self-assurance and has difficulty believing in anything (Young 1993; Jenkins 1995; Hutton 1996; see also Brown 1995). Its higher education system, buffeted by change in an era of rapid expansion followed by the 'consolidation' of the new era of the maximum aggregated student number (MASN), has problems about vision and long-term future. Ivory tower metaphors notwithstanding, universities live in, and off, their societies.

A national loss of purpose and confidence is exacerbated by division about our European political and privatized economic future. In this changing and uncertain world, higher education is called upon to meet multiple, seemingly incompatible, objectives. It is a context of declining resources and increasing uncertainty about resources in the immediate and longer-term future. Small wonder if in an atmosphere of crisis management and impending threat, vision withers and aspiration narrows down to small short-term objectives largely determined by others: well might the newly appointed vice chancellor have difficulty, up to the waist in alligators and sinking fast, remembering that the idea on appointment was to drain the swamp.

In 1996 the *fin de siècle* spirit for higher education is one of impending disaster, rather than the millennial utopianism for which not only politicians might have hoped. The confrontation between the vice chancellors and the government early in 1996 over a possible £300 student levy, leading to the appointment of a Committee of Inquiry into Higher Education (Secretary of State for Education and Employment 1996), bought political respite to carry past an impending election, but also raised expectations about a review similarly ambitious to that of Lord Robbins which was created 35 years earlier, in what with hindsight look to have been much easier and more hopeful times.

Reductionism is a longer-term matter than the impact of consolidation and the Chancellor of the Exchequer's last budget; but it is not unrelated to the impoverishment of vision. 'Lifelong learning', with the related concepts of the learning society and the learning organization, is commonly shrunk down to something much smaller. It is reductionist if the focus of 'learning' is moved from the society or organization exclusively to the individuals within it. It is reductionist also when the educational agenda shrinks to something close to skills training. Third, it is reductionist for the idea of the university to be equated with a service to meet consumers' economics-based skill-learning needs on demand. Cumulatively these forms of reductionist fragmentation produce a mean and wholly individualistic notion of the curriculum, the university and society. The whole person living in a social, cultural, civic and political system becomes economic 'man': a one-dimensional producer and consumer.

The context for considering a lifelong curriculum

Abolition of the binary division within higher education between universities on the one hand and polytechnics and colleges on the other was accompanied by a change of state in higher education, commonly characterized as the transition from an elite to a mass model. It is not always remembered that Martin Trow postulated a third, universal, phase: the first transition might be at an age participation rate (APR) of around 15 per cent, the second of around 50 per cent (Trow 1973). Note that this omits the larger part of the student population. More than half of UK university students now are adults by the normal criteria employed to distinguish them from pre-experience adults. The distinction between initial and, in its broadest post-experience sense, continuing education students is relevant to consideration of a lifelong curriculum.

In the early 1990s the system looked set to move through a mass towards a universal phase within a couple of decades. By 1995 it was maintained that some 60 per cent of the adult population were already engaged in higher education at one time or another, a statistic later contested. There is a well established pattern. Those with successful and usually therefore also enjoyable sustained initial education are the main 'consumers' of post-initial or continuing education – unto them that hath, more is given, and by them it is taken. The Confederation of British Industry has pressed for the government age participation target of 30 per cent set by Kenneth Baker as Secretary of State for Education (Baker 1989) to be raised to 40 and perhaps 50 per cent. Rapid expansion through the late 1980s and early 1990s, implying an uncapped commitment to rising public expenditure in the current student and institutional funding regime, was, however, replaced by the MASN referred to above: a straitjacket whereby institutions are penalized for going above as well as below target for full-time funded student numbers. Public expenditure can thus be better regulated. Progress towards a universal system is in the process halted. Hard on the heels of the MASN came an amplified debate about quality and standards fuelled by a later Secretary of State, John Patten. Some would have it that in the mid-1990s expansion should cease because the national pool of talent of those capable of benefiting from higher education has suddenly been drained.

The APR is an incomplete measure of the level and nature of participation in higher education. In APR terms the gallop from elite towards universal higher education has been halted. In terms of the issues raised in the opening paragraph of this section, the changeover from a binary to a unitary higher education system is by no means as clear-cut or stable as the merging of the sectors and their funding might suggest (Schuller 1995).

The 1990s introduced an era of competitive league tables in school and higher education: integration is accompanied by more sophisticated transparent differentiation using multiple performance measures. This is contested territory. Some measures cancel each other out: for instance, A level entry scores versus value added. Others are ambiguously and variously interpreted, such as the proportion of first class honours degrees, which is seen as a sign of both rising and falling standards. In this evolving competitive situation hierarchical groupings of universities jostle over status and membership. The 'R–X–T' (research, mixed, teaching only) divisions proposed and dismissed in the late 1980s seem to be re-emerging from competitive research (from the mid-1980s) and teaching (from the early 1990s) assessment exercises. The unitary system looks, prospectively, more like a three or four division football league. The first division may be an international class of some half dozen universities or the larger 'Russell group'.

It is in fact more complicated still. The colleges of higher education are part of the higher education system by funding, but not by title or status. In a conference presentation in 1995, Sir Christopher Ball foresaw a thousand British universities before the end of the twenty-first century. For the moment the title and status are guarded both by the old and ancient universities and by some newcomers who would kick away the ladder after boarding the vessel. Even the term 'university college' is controversial. The higher education system is thus still 'binary': universities, the territory of the Committee of Vice Chancellors and Principals (CVCP); and colleges, the territory of the smaller Standing Conference of Principals (SCOP).

More important is the 'new binary line' between the whole higher education institutional sector (CVCP and SCOP) and the further education sector, funded in England by a separate Further Education Funding Council (FEFC) alongside the Higher Education Funding Council for England (HEFCE). Through a variety of collaborative arrangements and partnerships, such as franchising and validation, the amount of higher education undertaken in the FE sector steadily increased, to the point where HEFCE felt obliged in 1995 to conduct an inquiry into the subject designed to uncover stakeholder attitudes to the phenomenon (HEFCE 1995). This new binary divide will eventually be removed. It may be slowly dissolved or more brutally swept away, as the UK continues to follow North American tendencies, and there is likely to be significant resistance before this happens. The Chief Executive of the HEFC for Wales predicted in a 1995 conference presentation that it might be a decade before the further and higher education funding systems merged – although cross-fertilization in methodology is already evident in Wales, and prospectively also in England. If and when merger occurs England may be seen to have crossed the second threshold and psychological barrier from elite through mass and into universal higher education.

It is relevant to the concept of 'lifelong' learning that the tendency to dissolve and regroup extends back to the 14 to 19 age span and curriculum. The FE–HE distinction has become fuzzy, also affecting part of the school system. Sixth form colleges joined the FE sector, destabilizing structures and market shares for upper secondary education, and blurring the boundaries which determine where adults (often thought of too narrowly as the only lifelong learners) attend for education. In 1996 the idea gained currency that university courses might also be taken in secondary schools, accelerating the passage of bright youngsters to academic adulthood (see, for example, *Times Higher Education Supplement* 1996).

Debates about the appropriate curriculum, in terms of relevance, core skills, vocationalization, competencies, work experience and workplace learning, likewise spill over, flowing back into early adolescence and for some, like Rover Learning Business, to still earlier years of childhood, which is where it is perceived that unhelpful dichotomies repugnant to lifelong learning first take root. From this perspective the dichotomy between school and the 'real world' is harmful, whether in primary school or at university. Rover seeks to be a 'learning organization', with its own lifelong curriculum, developed and delivered in partnership with other learning organizations outside the company. Thus, to conclude this discussion about its context, the lifelong curriculum of higher education cannot be contained entirely within the university, nor indeed within the formal education system: despite great resistance the reach of the university and its lifelong curriculum will have to come to extend lifelong and society-wide.

Discourse

It is tempting to pepper text with quotation marks, distancing oneself and reducing the discomfort that goes with using the modern discourse which has invaded education and, for instance, health policy debate. Internal and external markets, competition, clients, internal and external customers, consumers, input, throughput and output. Cost centres, supply chains, human resources and their management, downsizing and outsourcing. Value-added, performance measures and indicators, total quality management, benchmarking, world class, not to mention (*faute de mieux* for the modern university) just-in-time (see also Duke 1992: Chapter 2, and the discussion of the industrialization of the language of education in the introductory chapter of this volume).

The list continues to grow, sensibility to be dulled. In the mid-1980s even to refer to mission statement was to court ribaldry. A decade later the audible and written quote marks around these terms have faded. Is the commercialization of language a necessary accompaniment to a commodification of education (or should I say provision and delivery systems)? If the cultural shift in higher education is accurately measured by this change in discourse, and by the disappearance of apologetic quotation marks, then visionary ideas of a university in an era of lifelong learning have a poor prognosis indeed. Such discourse reduces vision for education: from the nurturing of growth to the moving of merchandise.

Quality and standards: does more mean worse?

The 'access movement', like feminism, has undergone two phases of resistance. In the early days (Access courses started at the beginning of the 1980s) there was soon anxiety about dilution of standards, and protection of that significantly finite, anti-lifelong learning mark of the gold standard, the classified honours degree. For a decade it was superficially allowed that more might mean different rather than worse (Ball 1990). Meanwhile, the 'access movement' emphasized the difference between 'more access' and 'wider access' (Fulton 1989). Expansion into the adult population was deemed to be about bringing the socially and educationally excluded into universities. It was not merely, as some feared (see, for instance, Wagner 1990), filling a gap created by smaller cohorts of 18-year-olds coming through the school system with the kind of folk who just missed out, mainly because, when they were younger, in many middle-class families 'girls did not go to university' (Pascall and Cox 1993).

The standards debate has returned with a vengeance. The Higher Education Quality Council (HEQC) is owned by CVCP and SCOP. Its political *raison d'être* is to keep quality assurance within the peer scrutiny of higher education institutions, and to hold government and its quangos, the funding councils, distant from the detail of the delivered curriculum. Most significant for the 'lifelong curriculum' may be an underlying tendency represented by the effort to assure the nation and specifically the Department for Education and Employment and the Treasury that standards are being maintained in the expanded system. If we move towards a national curriculum for higher education, will this be the same as a lifelong learning curriculum, or something quite different?

The HEQC was charged by Secretary of State for Education John Patten with looking at standards as well as quality. Ironically, the classification of teaching quality as usually 'satisfactory' (the majority, between those found to be excellent and the tiny handful deemed 'unsatisfactory') caused an overseas image and marketing problem, 'satisfactory' being a weak marketing term. Universities were already caught in a bind over home students: to make do with fewer resources year by year, or to admit that damage was occurring, and so to admit to declining standards (or lower quality) under the pressure of market competition and less to work with per student, thus inviting yet more interference. The diversification of the nominally unified university system ('all the way from Cambridge to Luton') posed an unanswerable question about the common standard of the 'British honours degree'. Where were the emperor's clothes?

In the late summer of 1995 the reinvigorated standards debate acquired a life of its own, especially when it was revealed that the school-leaver intake to universities included science and engineering students with poor school results. (Institutions failing to meet target student numbers, especially in these subject areas, suffer severe financial penalties through 'clawback' of part of their teaching grant.) In the absence of new resources coming into the much expanded system – meaning that students would contribute more directly via fees in the already semi-privatized system – it became easier to agree that all legitimate demand was already being met, and that further expansion was not needed. Collusion between politicians and vice chancellors proved short-lived, but for the moment such an alliance looked possible. However, the 1995 budget, which, probably by mistake, removed much of the universities' capital line for the next year, almost immediately provoked new confrontation, with threatened reduction of intake or a £300 levy on newly enrolling students by vice chancellors in a game of raising the stakes. In the event the crisis was defused by the announcement of a new

'Dearing commission' to look into higher education, and especially its funding (Secretary of State for Education and Employment 1996), while HEQC continued its 'graduateness' inquiry into standards in higher education.

This second wave of critical anxiety about quality in general and standards more sharply and specifically impinges upon our consideration of a lifelong curriculum. In the wake of the National Curriculum for schools, the idea of a national curriculum in higher education has gained currency in a mass system riddled by anxiety and self-doubt about standards. Buried beneath the short-term problems of coping with an administration wedded to free market privatization, yet prone to interfere in the minutiae of institutional behaviour, there is a larger question about the nature of the emergent curriculum of higher education. Will a lifelong perspective be sacrificed to a core curriculum for the young, which is intended to assure that all those graduating from higher education have gained, and can give, value for money?

Thus, by 1996 the standards debate had been reinvigorated rather than exhausted. By its very nature it is an unwinnable, and unsolvable, contest in which many data can be used to demonstrate diametrically opposed positions. Debate about core curriculum, transferable skills, competences and outcomes likewise remained vigorous but often confused. It too was politically and ideologically driven. The impact of the Teaching and Learning Technology Programme of the HEFCE was still being evaluated, but did not point out a short or easy road to large economies through common materials used in distant and self-directed modes. None the less, learning and learner-centredness, supported by 'learning resource centres', was winning ground against 'traditional', labour-intensive, tutorial-based teaching: learner self-reliance (the 'learning to learn' of the lifelong learning persuasion) became a newly discovered virtue fed by economic necessity. As demand continued for demonstrated attainment of threshold standards, with higher education pressed by professional associations, consumer interests and awarding bodies, the idea of a core undergraduate curriculum began to look not entirely fanciful.

Graduating and 'graduateness'

The idea of graduating to an inalienable status (a 'first class Oxford man') is out of sorts with the idea of lifelong learning; with the fact that adults must and do continue to learn and change as their world changes, through most of their life; and with the facts of technological change and the obsolescence of knowledge, skills and cultural attitudes and values. Does one become a 'master' of economics or engineering for ever more, or demonstrate a particular masterly competence at the time of taking this degree? The same criticism can be levelled against the vocational qualifications system of National and General National Vocational Qualifications growing up alongside the academic: demonstrating competence to perform in a

unit of assessment to a specified level does not guarantee one's performance next year, even if the unit is still relevant to next year's technology and
needs (see Hyland 1994).

HEQC has developed the idea, through the term 'graduateness', that
there may be identified something which captures the essence of higher
education and which graduating guarantees. This might mean a threshold
standard containing elements – a curriculum core – of personal transferable skills favoured by competence approaches to the curriculum. It may
not necessarily imply greatly altering the content of the curriculum, but
rather finding new ways of describing what it contains in terms of intellectual and other skills, and underpinning knowledge.

The difficulty from the perspective of lifelong learning lies in the notion
of a common standard gained at one moment (the graduation ceremony;
at some stage in the final honours year?) which somehow gives a distinguishing finite quality of 'graduateness'. Life and learning are messier. Such
a response to the demand for fixed and common standards in a changing
and varied world puts aside the ideas of recurrency in education to support
lifelong learning; puts aside even the abiding importance, hard as it is to
operationalize, of a continuing, persisting, core 'learning to learn' competence, skill or facility.

Rather than try to snare the 'core skill' of 'learning to learn', let us instead consider whether there is emerging a 'university lifelong curriculum'.

Tertiary or lifelong?

If the term tertiary had not already gained specific narrow meaning it might
by now have come to embrace a third level of education, which is culturally
though not legally compulsory for the expanded middle classes and those
aspiring to join them. Graduating, a threshold standard for tertiary, first
level, degree education, would be virtually a prerequisite for regular employment in the formal economy. The two-year associate degree (see, for
instance, Robertson 1994) and the two-year equivalent post-secondary level
4 GNVQ floated for discussion by the National Council for Vocational
Qualifications in 1995 share the idea of a quasi-mandatory threshold.

In the 1970s some Australians used the term 'quaternary' to refer to
levels beyond the first degree: further and higher education following a
break from initial full-time education, at whatever level. Such purposes and
provision are now called '(post-experience) continuing education'. As the
review of postgraduate education initiated by HEFCE in 1995 should reveal,
the purposes, modes and clienteles embraced by taught master's degrees
include a wealth of lifelong learning in the form of updating and the
acquisition of new knowledge and skills. The post-experience MBA is an
obvious example of lateral diversification. These are quite distinct from
completion of the initial cycle of basic education prior to entering the
workplace seriously, in the form of the new four-year, or 'three plus one',

master's degrees which enhance relative employability as the proportion of each cohort entering initial higher education rises; or a more specialized year of study to tool up to the level of vocational ability required to enter more and more specific sectors of employment.

In other words, the initial 'non-lifelong' curriculum may be lengthened for reasons of relative or absolute advantage: competition in a crowded labour market or to gain essential prerequisite knowledge and skills. The master's degree has become hugely diverse. With modularization, distance, work-based, electronic and other mixed modes, it is a highly flexible means of accrediting university study which straddles and confuses any distinction between initial and continuing – or recurrent or lifelong – education. Is this another threat to quality? Or is it a sign that a lifelong curriculum is being adopted in a broader sense than was used above, albeit under pressure of market forces rather than from visionary planning?

Selling higher education short: a new '*trahison des clercs*'?

The theme of this chapter is reductionism and poverty of vision. The innuendo in this sub-heading is that academic intellectuals, and their leaders in the universities, may be guilty of collusion, cowardice or at the least lack of energy to develop ambitious and generous visions as pressure to survive gets more acute.

The very ploy foreshadowed above, to split 'tertiary' from lifelong, is one form of such betrayal. In defining post-experience continuing education as the lifelong realm one would be abandoning prospective gains to the larger higher or post-school system offered by the perspective of lifelong learning. Since university continuing education is now meant to be integrated or 'mainstreamed', this is anyway an insecure refuge. It would be short-sighted of university teachers oriented to a traditional 18-plus clientele to neglect the needs and opportunities represented by 'non-traditional' learners seeking higher education; and equally short-sighted for those in university continuing education to draw too sharp a distinction between the aspirations and needs of the young and of older, post-experience, students.

One form of collusion can be for universities to agree to take more business, to keep young people off the streets and out of an overcrowded labour market, in return for some modest increase in resources short of matching the increase in student numbers. This is one way of observing the events from the late 1980s to the mid-1990s. It is not entirely plausible, however, since there is also a widely held and deep commitment among many in higher education to widening access for economic, but also perhaps more vigorously for social, reasons. The 11-plus scholarship generation is now in office, and not without memories and ideals.

If there is failure of courage and vision, it lies rather in the wish not to grapple with the possibility of the more fundamental change in the curriculum which the 'lifelong curriculum' must imply. It would imply taking seriously the difficult business of engaging with 'industry' in the broadest sense – all kinds of enterprises and employment sites, private and public, community and non-governmental groups and bodies – to develop a *curriculum* – a *course* of learning experiences – which would connect academic study more closely with the society, including the workplaces, to which young students hope to move and from which, increasingly, older part-time students come. The lack of interest in or hostility to higher level GNVQs by many in the now massive education industry is one manifestation of conservatism, protectionism or *trahison*.

Does a 'lifelong curriculum' have any meaning?

Learning for the whole length and breadth of life differs from what are commonly taken to be the post-initial educational opportunities proposed by OECD at the beginning of the 1970s as 'recurrent education'; yet recurrent education was conceived and described as a strategy for lifelong learning (OECD 1973). The vision of recurrent education has since sometimes been emasculated (not by OECD): reduced to little more than periodic retraining.

The lifelong perspective offers a way of critiquing and revising all levels and areas of the curriculum so as to foster a propensity, willingness and ability to go on learning; to seek deliberate educational support where self-directed learning does not suffice. It implies examining the nature of knowledge and the nature of learning more carefully and deliberately than is our wont. It brings centrally into consideration 'the reflective practitioner' in all walks of life: the active citizen; participatory workplace and other democracy; 'tacit knowledge'. Its message is as clear, albeit as politically unfashionable, for early years schooling as for higher education. Here the implication is to foster attitudes and skills conducive to continuous critical inquiry rather than just the obvious knowledge and skill acquisitions: process rather than only content.

In higher education, elements of the Employment Department's Enterprise in Higher Education initiative get close to reviewing the curriculum, in its larger learning-experience sense, from this perspective. Core transferable skills are part of the agenda for a lifelong curriculum. Not surprisingly, one aspect, off-putting to some initially, was closer partnership with industry. This meant looking beyond the walls to ask what students needed to know and do, and what they needed to be like, in the life after study. The lifelong curriculum implies closer integration of the university with the community than the English university has typically felt comfortable with in recent times. It does not mean being 'market-driven' as the system now only supposedly is. Rather it means taking as the reference point for curriculum design and revision the diverse, confusing world on which the university feeds, and co-designing lifelong curricula which build on the special expertise and the special, semi-detached situation of the university, exploiting these to provide a 'learning experience' calculated to produce active lifelong learners whose academic learning naturally connects with and applies to life outside that institution. This does not work for the society, the system or the individual institution as long as the government is a quasi-monopoly purchaser.

Approached thus, 'the lifelong curriculum' becomes infused with meaning for initial as well as for post-experience higher education. The two kinds of learning situation differ somewhat, and will continue to do so even though the literally full-time undergraduate will become little more than a memory. None the less, adopting a lifelong perspective will help us to reconceptualize and reinstate sandwich, known in some other systems as cooperative, education; to re-energize practice-based learning for teachers, nurses, doctors and others; and to bring work-based learning and its accreditation more confidently into the heartland of each university and its curriculum. What this points towards is not a core 'subject' curriculum so much as core characteristics, qualities and kinds of outcomes for all who enter and re-enter higher education.

Learning organizations and societies?

It may seem distinctly odd to criticize a discussion of the lifelong curriculum as reductionist for taking cognizance only of the learning of individuals. Given historical and philosophical associations between the notions of lifelong learning and 'the learning society', however, we need to consider how these two connect in looking towards the higher education system of the future. A learning organism or organization is one which can read, analyse, adapt to, act on and interact with its environment. Changed behaviour is the expected outcome and sign of learning. In speaking of lifelong and learning we tend to shift attention towards 'real life' adaptation, learning from mistakes, learning life's lessons, and away from passing examinations. The units-of-assessment approach is an attempt to reflect such a change. Within a lifelong curriculum the dichotomy between learning from experience and learning in the classroom is reduced: 'experiential learning' in its various senses is already a growth area, and the accreditation of prior and work-based learning is beginning to invade the academic curriculum and the assessment repertoire.

Intellectual repugnance at the idea of an organization learning appears to have receded (Jones and Hendry 1992). The concept is familiar and expresses a sought-after state of perfection among leading industrial corporations. The 'learning society' causes another kind of problem, possibly because of connotations of the Europe of the 1930s, in which an organic nation was greater and became more highly valued than the component parts – its citizens (Duke 1995). There is arguably a sense in which only the individual can learn; traditions of liberal individualism make us suspicious of any larger organic entity. With or without calculation, Thatcherite individualism has taken advantage of this liberal sensitivity, to the point of asserting the non-existence of society altogether. If glorifying and personifying the organic state or *Volk* is one dangerous fallacy, at the other extreme there is the reductionist fallacy. Lifelong learning implies a curriculum in context. Whether or not the terms find favour, it implies living and working in learning organizations as elements in a learning society, and preparing people for these. Societies and organizations which do not learn experience atrophy and death.

A more obvious set of implications concerns the formal curriculum of higher education. Students who 'graduate' into a learning society need the aptitudes and capabilities to live and contribute there. They need to be able to problematize, resolve and work out how to be a part of that 'society'. Is it the political state? Depending where they live and identify, is it the United Kingdom, England or Scotland? What about more regional and local identities? Are they also, perhaps primarily, becoming European citizens? They must learn to come to terms with the reality of multiple political memberships, including increasingly the idea of membership of an interdependent global 'community' with new forms of political and legal manifestation. Is it primarily political or civic membership and identity to which the 'learning society' refers? What needs to happen to empower the student to feel part and to be an active part of his or her society? What need you learn and must you be able to do – and feel – to contribute to societal learning? What are the skills of civic and political participation, and where do they appear in the curriculum of higher education? It will be necessary to keep asking and answering these questions to sustain a relevant and effective lifelong learning curriculum.

It is similar with the learning organization. Students will 'graduate' to become members, employees, customers or victims. An increasing number of corporations now call their employees associates. 'Associate', curiously, seeks not to marginalize employees but to enhance their status as members and co-owners in a psychological sense. It is congruent with, if not a stated manifestation of, the idea of a learning organization.

A less obvious implication for the lifelong curriculum is that the university itself becomes a learning organization and not simply an organization in which learning takes place. One manifestation of reductionism apropos 'the learning organization' is to equate it with encouraging members to learn, usually by going on courses or 'doing' staff development. The concept of the hidden curriculum is more relevant. The total environment and experience created and provided by the university is often more powerful and generative of learning than any written curriculum. We are more conscious of this in some areas, such as ethnic and gender behaviour, harassment and environmentalism, than in others.

How conscious are we apropos teaching styles of what students learn through them about authority, autonomy and responsibility? How far are self-directed learning and independence of thought and tested judgement part of the teaching strategy, other than where paucity of time and resources dictate ingenious means of saving teaching labour? What do students perceive, experience and internalize about forms of rewarded, unrewarded and perhaps subtly punished behaviours? What kind of learning environment do they experience through encounter with those other than teaching staff on the institutional payroll, and with teaching staff in roles other than that of teacher?

These questions are about making and sustaining a scholarly culture in higher education (Barnett 1990). They are also about creating a 'learning environment' in which students as learners are enabled to develop judgements, test behaviour, discover consequences and gain in the skills, confidence and ability needed to exercise the many facets of their personalities and potential required of a multiplicity of life roles in the learning society. These are civic, domestic, social and cultural roles as well as the roles of employee-producer and consumer. They apply with obvious force to the 'tertiary', still usually full-time, youngster living away from home for the first substantial period of time and undergoing a rite of passage. They can be as important for the first-time, second-chance, access-type adult immortalized as Rita; but also for other older people coming back to gain a higher qualification or more advanced knowledge and skills, with much at stake in terms of forging a new professional, but perhaps also personal, identity, often covert and unacknowledged. The university provides a partly protected space for personal transformation, as those who teach the post-experienced well know.

The hidden curriculum of the school refers, for example, to the messages pupils pick up from teachers' behaviour about what really matters. Especially telling is the match or mismatch between precept and example. While this is important it also makes an implicit statement about organizational functioning. The university manifests and unwittingly teaches how an organization functions or malfunctions in terms of its own reflective practice. What mechanisms exist to enable it to learn from its experience and adapt its behaviour accordingly, such as staff–student liaison committees, examination and review boards, staff meetings and informal professional dialogue? How do all its members learn to take part in the activities which enable the organization intelligently to adapt its behaviour? Is knowledge-gathering and intelligence demonstrated to reside in just a few senior individuals who exercise power based in their organizational positions? Is the university open and absorbing information through all its pores, processing and acting on the information thus received, or is this left to the boss (compare Price 1994)? Is it ahead of the games governments and universities play, or constantly wrong-footed? Is it in good heart, with a shared sense of mission, purpose, values and direction, or divided against itself and centrifugally fragmented?

Indicators of the kind suggested here reveal whether or not a university is a learning organization as well as a deliberate teaching and assessing one.

A university which is a vigorous learning organization is also likely to be obviously and actively concerned with its teaching and learning support strategies for students, and with 'human resource development' strategies for its staff; but these are measures and by-products of being a learning organization rather than definers of that condition. Temporary members of an effective learning organization, students, short-term research staff and teaching fellows are likely to learn something about active participation, to find ways of contributing their own understanding and experience, and seeing it taken aboard as relevant intelligence; in short, to be somewhat encouraged and empowered to participate, however modestly, in the wider learning society. They will have experienced part of the 'lifelong curriculum' and are more likely to become active and responsible citizens as a result.

Universities in a learning society

Turning from the interior life of universities to their contribution as organizational members of a learning society identifies a final set of questions: about *their* active and responsible 'citizenship'. It is a fashionable heresy to consider the modern university as a holding company in which the various subsidiaries trade, cooperate and compete much like other commercial enterprises. The whole is then no more than the sum of its parts: in an ideal model the whole scarcely exists except as a flag of trading convenience. This is another manifestation of *le trahison des clercs*: the denial, because it is difficult to sustain in postmodern times, of an idea of a university which distinguishes it from other trading enterprises. Management models and metaphors have a way of gaining a life of their own. Handy and challenging heuristic devices gallop away with the essence of the university, whatever is enshrined in its statement of mission.

The moral high ground is not comfortable to occupy. It became less comfortable during the Thatcher years. Some in British universities, not just social scientists, have exercised a function of social criticism which is by its nature conflictual. Not all politicians are high-minded, tolerant Voltairians. Highmindedness went out of fashion in the 1980s. Before that the universities had been discredited, blamed for what was perceived as both economic and social failure in the crises of the early 1970s. Academic freedom is much-valued, and also abused. The lesser abuse is its use as an excuse to avoid accountability. The greater abuse lies not in government interference but in a failure to take risks: the failure to exercise, however courteously yet firmly, the duty to inquire, and to share the results of academic inquiry, controversial or politically unpopular as they may be. The moral base for the existence of the university is honest, challenging and disinterested teaching, and dissemination of the results of free inquiry, now more commonly known as research and publication.

In a commonly homogenized, mass production and consumption society, which includes the mass production and consumption of most specifically identified 'culture' and entertainment, universities have the opportunity and the duty, by virtue of their charters, to offer alternatives: other views, other arguments, other values. In a time of great transience and instability they are also refuges for the conservation of alternatives as well as for the conservation of various artefacts, including various knowledges. The visualization and creation of alternatives is not in contradiction to the function of conservation. We are increasingly aware of the utility, ethics apart, of preserving the diversity of species – if only because we do not yet know which we will later need, which we will later discover how to exploit. Universities are museums and cathedrals for the preservation and valuing of scarce knowledge, unfashionable disciplines and perspectives. Intellectual biodiversity is sustained in part by the continuing diversity of subjects, schools and sub-disciplines through which young and older students pass for exposure or immersion.

Thinking at a societal level then, the lifelong curriculum within the university system should be lifewide in content, reflecting and transmitting the diversity of intellectual inheritance, knowledge, understanding and experience. Especially as long as the HEQC's emergent 'threshold standards' are sustained through some kind of core 'process' curriculum, it matters only that new and older members of society continue to flow in at least threshold numbers through the many places and ways of seeing and knowing, to ensure that few if any are lost. Our national ecosystem, as a learning society, requires biodiversity. The university is an element in this life-chain. Reduced to brokering relations between an aggregation of competing cost centres where the weakest perish, it ceases to be special and different. Vision contracts to the business education scheme and private finance initiative.

In a society which builds few cathedrals, the university is needed all the more, alongside and representing values different from those of its other major artefacts: the sports stadium, the leisure centre, the out-of-town shopping complex. This is not just a matter of diversity of knowledge-forms and values, subjects or disciplines. There is also the division of powers among the great estates of the realm. The university stands here alongside the judiciary, the media and also the market.

Squaring the circle: lifelong learning and quality in a mass system

Can quality as well as diversity be sustained in a mass system of higher education? A new threat to the university system is destruction from within. It will be ironic if when it occurs the long overdue feminization of the professoriate merely reflects its diminished status. More tragic yet will be the result if those formerly excluded who now find their way into university feel seriously cheated. If their achievement feels hollow they may be tempted to blame the obvious suspect – the university and its faculty – and to diminish or destroy its works.

Clearly the modern university system, excluding the ancient, still prestigious universities and a few others jostling for position, cannot deliver to its students the privilege that a very selective system virtually assured all its graduates two generations ago (see Brown 1995 on cultural capital and social exclusion). Quality and relevance of learning experience can be secured in a mass system. Privileged access to well found positions for all who graduate clearly cannot. Instead, graduating may quickly become a prerequisite for entry to the less insecure, albeit often humble, parts of the changing labour market.

A potentially benevolent cycle of quality, relevance, accessibility and social utility might become a circle squared, through the development of community university networks, the tracings of which may already be discerned in many parts of the country. One such example is the Warwick Community University Board, with its nine further education partners: this is not an agenda exclusively for the 'new universities'. Liaisons taking place in the mid-1990s across the new binary line between further and higher education represent astute preventative measures as learning organizations anticipate changes in which policy-makers of whatever political affiliation insist upon greater regional planning, coordination and delivery in a more vocationally oriented system.

Partnership between educational institutions as well as between education and industry represents one means of managing, and managing in, an uncertain environment. Partnerships can marry further education's strengths of local accessibility, market intelligence and user-friendliness with the university's national and international standing. The next expansion of higher education, when new funding modes are created, and growth towards universal higher education resumes, could well be of higher within further education, allowing progression to a local, or if needs be to a nonlocal, university campus.

If the English retain virtue, it is of pragmatism, moderation and compromise. A community university system would remove the leaky membrane separating further from higher education and allow the continuation of intimacy in higher education through face-to-face encounter in what would still, by world standards, be small university communities. This would exercise the pragmatic gene. In the process it could move the system away from reductionism towards a more organic synthesis and symbiosis: towards an attainable and thoroughly worthwhile vision of a learning university through which the lifelong curriculum can be nurtured and continuously renewed.

References

Baker, K. (1989) *Higher Education – 25 Years on* (speech at the University of Lancaster, press notice). London, Department of Education and Science.

Ball, C. (1990) *More Means Different. Widening Access to Higher Education*. London, RSA.

Barnett, R. (1990) *The Limits of Competence. Knowledge, Higher Education and Society.* Buckingham, Open University Press/SRHE.

Brown, P. (1995) Cultural capital and social exclusion: some observations on recent trends in education, employment and the labour market, *Work, Employment and Society,* 9, 1.

Committee of Vice Chancellors and Principals (1996) Lifetime learning: CVCP Response, press release. London, CVCP.

Department for Education and Employment (1995) *Lifetime Learning: a Consultation Document.* Sheffield, DfEE.

Duke, C. (1992) *The Learning University. Towards a New Paradigm?* Buckingham, Open University Press/SRHE.

Duke, C. (1995) Metaphors of learning, *Adults Learning,* 6(10), 300–2.

European Commission (1995) *Teaching and Learning. Towards a Learning Society.* Brussels, European Commission.

Fulton, O. (ed.) (1989) *Access and Institutional Change.* Buckingham, Open University Press/SRHE.

Higher Education Funding Council for England (1995) *Funding the Relationship: Higher Education in Further Education Colleges.* Bristol, HEFCE.

Hutton, W. (1996) *The State We're In.* London, Vintage.

Hyland, T. (1994) *Competence, Education and NVQs: Dissenting Perspectives.* London, Cassell.

Jenkins, S. (1995) *Accountable to None.* London, Hamish Hamilton.

Jones, A. M. and Hendry, C. (1992) *The Learning Organisation: a Review of Literature and Practice.* London, HRD Partnership.

OECD (1973) *Recurrent Education: a Strategy for Lifelong Learning.* Paris, OECD.

Pascall, G. and Cox, R. (1993) *Women Returning to Higher Education.* Buckingham, Open University Press/SRHE.

Price, C. (1994) Piloting higher education chance: a view from the helm, in S. Weil (ed.) *Introducing Change from the Top.* London, Kogan Page.

Robertson, D. (1994) *Choosing to Change.* London, HEQC.

Schuller, T. (ed.) (1995) *The Changing University?* Buckingham, Open University Press/SRHE.

Secretary of State for Education and Employment (1996) *Statement to the House of Commons 19 February 1996. Appointment of National Committee of Inquiry into Higher Education.* London, DfEE.

Times Higher Education Supplement (1996) Colleges plan to enrol children, *THES,* 5 April.

Trow, M. (1973) *Problems in the Transition from Elite to Mass Higher Education.* Berkeley, CA, Carnegie Commission on Higher Education.

Wagner, L. (1990) Adults in higher education: the next five years, *Adults Learning,* 2(4), 94–6.

Young, H. (1993) *One of Us.* London, Pan.

5

Social Justice in a Learning Market

David Robertson

Background

Universities in the UK are being swung through an arc of change. In common with other services in the public domain, they are being exposed to unaccustomed forces: quasi-market and near-market machinery; demands for greater efficiency, quality and value-for-money; and new managerialist techniques which challenge academic values and professional cultures. The overall increase in competitive pressure, manifested largely in proxy form by expenditure squeezes and additional regulatory control rather than by competition for students, is steadily changing the character of professional life in higher education. How far this is yielding better universities, higher quality academic performance, enhanced national effectiveness or greater social justice remains highly contested.

In this assessment, I want to argue that the old bargain between universities and the state has effectively broken down. The state is no longer prepared to support a higher education sector from public taxation alone to pursue objectives over which the state has traditionally chosen to exercise little direct control. Instead, the state has been engaged over the past decade in defining a new contract with higher education and policies towards the sector have been bent to that purpose. In this new contract, either the state will exercise greater control over the character of higher education or universities will need to find alternative sources of support if they are to maintain their sovereignty. It is possible that both will need to occur before a new bargain is established.

I should add, before going any further, that the ambitions of the state are not entirely unreasonable. The old bargain had become unsustainable and a recasting of the relationship has been inevitable for some time. It is wholly predictable that the state in the latter part of the twentieth century should look to its higher education sector for more than a selective or incidental contribution to national well-being. Higher education constitutes a major investment in competitive advantage for any society, but the success with which universities have sustained to date a particular kind of social and economic formation in the UK is no guarantee that similar success will be reproduced in the vastly changed conditions of the next century.

Accordingly, universities in the UK are slowly being modernized and brought within the fold of civil society. Participation in UK higher education is becoming, as elsewhere in the world, a part of the welfare bargain individuals expect to reach with the state. Meanwhile, employers continue to expect universities to absorb some of the cost of research and innovation which would otherwise fall on themselves. Furthermore, while universities have always contributed directly to economic performance by the generation of new knowledge and applications, they are being required also to contribute more directly to labour force preparation. To this extent, a new bargain is being negotiated but in conditions which universities would not have chosen for themselves.

The question before us is simple: can universities define the characteristics of a 'new' bargain which would be acceptable to themselves as well as to other parties to the contract? Or must they stand to one side while the state takes the initiative and determines their future? These questions are highly pertinent in the context of the National Committee of Inquiry into Higher Education – the Dearing Review – and invite the higher education sector to ask searching questions of itself. To that end, this discussion seeks to analyse the collapse of the old bargain and reflect on some features which may appear in new arrangements.

Policy development: confusions and consistencies

A suggestion that policy on UK higher education over the past decade has followed anything like a straight line must confront the fact that, with distressing regularity, it has veered from one direction to another with little apparent consistency.

An obvious example of confusion concerns policies developed between 1989 and 1995 on the shape, size and purpose of the sector. One moment a course was set for expansion: government stimulated rising participation and the sector responded with increased student places and some imaginative proposals for change. Then, within a few years, expansion shuddered to a halt, innovators found themselves beached and institutions have gone into an approximation of financial free-fall. Meanwhile, attention has shifted from the benefits of sectoral growth for national competitiveness to the losses incurred in national reputation if quality and standards were to decline. A 'moral panic' has followed, in which access and openness, newly adopted by the sector as virtues only a year or so earlier, are being presented as threats to the quality of the system. Government policy has moved from an encouragement of diversity and flexibility among institutions and students to a stance which promises greater regulation and control. Students, once buoyed by promises of graduation, now face prospects of debt and employment uncertainty. And half the institutions in the sector, latterly decorated by the title 'university', now find themselves arraigned in the name of vocationalism on the charge of 'academic drift'.

While responsibility for these oscillations must lie in the last resort with policy-makers, it is difficult to avoid the impression that higher education has not been particularly adroit as a sector in securing for itself a position high enough up the political agenda to command either the concentration of policy-makers or the sympathy of the public at large. Consequently, policy emerges incoherently as the increasingly desperate efforts of both government and universities to manage financial pressures over the short term collide with longer-term imperatives.

Meanwhile, universities and government wrestle for control of the short-term political agenda. The former, lacking any recognizable mandate, turn for support to public opinion only to find that manifestations of concern have been muted by years of democratic exclusion from higher education. Relatively isolated by sustained indifference to popular opinion, universities in the UK are being left to negotiate a new bargain with the state in conditions which could have been avoided.

It is a principal contention of this discussion that, if universities had defined for themselves long ago a defining role in the supply of lifelong learning, they would now be better placed to assemble coalitions of support with which to take advantage of any confusion in the policy-making process. As it is, attempts by universities to maintain the quality of an ancient elite model in the context of increased participation and a restructured labour market are producing an unappealing hybridization of form and purpose. The sector turns inwards in search of intimacy and solace; while events beyond demand that universities face outwards to public accountability and responsiveness. The wider public looks on in confusion.

So the losses begin to accumulate: reductions in institutional autonomy; managerial constraints on academic freedom; an erosion of deference to academic authority; impatience with special pleading at a time when more accessible public services are faced with financial difficulties. Even authorities within the sector itself swing round and suggest that perhaps money spent on higher education might be spent on nursery education or post-school training, where the returns to investment are allegedly greater. When it costs £7000 of public money to educate a university student but less than £1000 for a primary school pupil, it is not altogether surprising that politicians on all sides should start to wonder whether there is as much advantage as received wisdom suggests in continuing to invest enormous sums of public money in a higher education sector so reluctant to change.

On the other hand, new opportunities are being created by the process of modernization which invite universities to change in ways they can accommodate without compromising their central purpose. These opportunities involve the formation of the kind of strategic alliances, with users and other client groups, which sustain other public services over the long term.

For it seems to be clear that the survival of the university in the form to which we have grown accustomed is no longer guaranteed. Universities, if they are to prosper in the future, must change *and* ally.

Accordingly, I want to argue somewhat against the grain of the interpretation which regards current policy-making in the sector as confused and inconsistent, or as a conspiracy against the interests of higher education. Although policy in the short term has varied unhelpfully, the policy 'long wave' has remained relatively constant. The enduring features are defined by the need to produce a strategic response to questions of the purpose of higher education in a modern society; to reach a settlement on the appropriate balance between public and private interests in matters of funding; to secure agreement on the relationship to be preferred between learners and institutional providers; and to achieve consensus on the role of higher education in assisting national economic effectiveness. These policy parameters are likely to remain in place until a 'new' bargain has been established.

Furthermore, although there is plenty of reason to believe that the state will continue to encroach on the sovereignty of universities, following the pattern of the past three decades (Salter and Tapper 1994), it is important to interpret this as much as an obligation it discharges in the national interest as a malign constraint on individual academic freedom. Indeed, as the terms of the 'new' bargain unfold, universities may be required to define more precisely what they mean by 'academic freedom' and how it should be safeguarded. It has been the task of other public services over the past 16 years to define what they value and regard as essential – their 'core business', if one can borrow from current management language – and universities may need to work on this question also.

From 'old' bargain to 'new' bargain: the challenge for the Dearing inquiry

Contemporary analysis of UK higher education must inevitably take into consideration the impact of the Dearing Committee. A body of this nature can provide a timely occasion for reflection, and can sometimes lead to far-reaching proposals and the formation of a new consensus. Judging by the terms of reference, this appears to be the intention, although the membership of the committee may yield altogether more pedestrian outcomes. Dearing has been charged to make recommendations on the shape, structure, size and funding of higher education sufficient to meet national needs for the next two decades or more. What is less clear is whether any subsequent consensus will be able to carry forward the changes which a modern system of higher education needs, or whether the review will simply marshall the vested interests of the sector into a cosmetic rearrangement of the past.

The Dearing Review does raise other questions. Why, for example, has the British government found it necessary to launch a major national

inquiry several years *after* two White Papers had already transformed legisla-
tion and institutional relationships across the sector (DES 1987, 1991), *after*
the massive expansion in participation since the late 1980s and *after* numerous policy reports on various aspects of the sector? The short-term answer
is that government appears to have been hustled into calling the inquiry by
exceptionally hostile reaction to the 1995 expenditure cuts and the threat
by universities to impose tuition fee charges. Its bipartisan character is
more a reflection of the awkwardness of the problems to be addressed, and
the lack of obvious political advantage to be obtained by a political party
which produces the appropriate solutions, particularly on funding.

Nevertheless, one must assume that government and opposition have in
mind a more elevated purpose than short-term political convenience. The
chance has been made available to produce a thoroughly radical agenda for
change in UK higher education, clarifying the confusions that exist, less in
the short-term policy process but more in the longer-term character and
direction of the sector.

The principal cause of the bewilderment is, as I have suggested above,
the collapse of the 'old bargain' under the terms of which universities have
been largely free to do as they choose, funded but unimpeded by a grateful
state. Now the funding is being withdrawn, and some of the gratitude also.
In its place a 'new' bargain is emerging, which seeks to tie higher education
more directly to national economic success within the context of national
standards and lifetime education and training targets. Furthermore, the
'new' bargain is founded on the premise that universities will need to cast
off their preoccupation with social exclusion and inward-facing accountability in favour of a place in the public arena, exposed both to the forces
which have substantially reshaped public services in the UK and to the
interests of a more extensive range of potential clients.

At the moment, it is not clear how well prepared universities are for this
new bargain. The frustratingly conservative character of higher education,
the fragmentation of the sector into a multiplicity of largely autonomous fief-
doms and the preference for self-referenced over public judgements of role
and purpose leave universities poorly placed to develop the coherent strategies which are needed if the 'new' bargain is to be negotiated successfully.

From work on an earlier occasion, I attempted to sketch out some of the
other problems which currently beset the sector: lack of confidence in a
sustained government commitment to student expansion in higher education; ambiguous signals from funding councils on the balance to be achieved
between teaching and research; a lack of consistency between priorities for
provision in higher education, the recruitment of students and the development of the national labour market; uncertainty over employer preferences for graduate outputs; and an ambiguous commitment to flexibility
and choice within the academic community. Overall, I suggested, we needed
to ask the question: what is higher education for? (Robertson 1994: 9–10).

In pursuing an answer to that question. I want to suggest that if the 'new'
bargain' for higher education is to be effective and sustainable, it must

involve a fundamental commitment to social justice and an acceptance that the pursuit of social justice is an arm of national effectiveness. For this mandate to be discharged successfully, higher education institutions will need to be modernized culturally, organizationally and politically. This type of transformation can best be realized within the context of a learning society in which participation in higher education becomes a natural part of the learning careers of most individuals. In a learning society which features universities as major assets, most people would enter higher education for some purpose at some time in their lives to gain reputable credentials for personal advancement, either in employment or more generally. When universities present themselves as public assets in this manner, it is more likely that they will be able to assemble coalitions of popular support for their longer-term security and prosperity.

A modern and effective system of higher education in the UK may be sustainable only in the context of a new multipartite 'bargain' between the state, universities, employers and learners. The old bargain, based on restricted state-sponsored access to a particular kind of cultural experience, will not do. It is affordable neither for the state nor for individuals; it no longer provides the means by which the national economy can maintain competitive advantage; and, above all, it is not fair.

A 'new' bargain begins with a commitment to social justice. Public institutions which are not defined in terms of social justice – accessible, accountable, fair to internal and external clients, responsive to public need – are not institutions which will easily attract support over the long term. On the other hand, public institutions which do not provide services that user groups require can find themselves replaced by other entrants to the service market. Until now this has been unthinkable in the case of higher education, but the development of new information networks and the growth in centres of expertise outside universities opens up the possibility that a new kind of learning market may be forming in which the campus-based residential university is merely one of a number of suppliers of higher education.

Under these conditions, the traditional university may retain an advantage because of quality, reputation and the character of its learning experience. However, it is unlikely to do so because of affordability or product character alone. Competitor providers – 'modernized' universities, other accredited bodies and so forth – would almost certainly seek to lower the costs of learning to the individual by increasing the choice and flexibility with which the learning 'product' could be obtained and lowering the investment costs from public and private sources. The traditional university would then face a two-pronged challenge from alternative suppliers in the learning market based on customized learning at lower costs to the individual.

To this end, the 'modern' university would couple competitive positioning within the learning market with a commitment to social justice – providing an affordable and accessible higher education for groups which would otherwise be excluded from universities. It would be in a position to form new alliances with students, communities and employers based on a commitment to meeting their service needs. And if the strategic alliances were successful, they would start to lay down the foundations of popular support and security which traditional universities are currently losing.

A learning market for the learning society: towards a new bargain?

It is impossible to assess at this stage how far the Dearing Review will go down the path of radical reform. One can anticipate that the outcomes will reflect the current consensus on funding and provide plenty of mood music on employment, vocationalism and the like. Thereafter, the big question for Dearing concerns the relationship the committee wishes to encourage between individual learners and institutional providers. Leaving this relationship unchanged will emasculate any other proposals on funding, quality or employment relevance.

Furthermore, subscribing to the rhetoric of a learning society will not be enough to produce the changes required, or to win public assent for extensive investment. A learning society drawn up in the image of educational providers alone does not guarantee the dynamism required to sustain it. Arrangements must be capable of adapting to different demands from a variety of participating interests. A learning society committed to social justice draws its vitality from diversity – that is, from the operation of an effective 'learning market' throughout post-secondary education. A learning market within a learning society appears to be the most obvious means by which higher education can assemble an adequate coalition of popular support to ensure continued investment from interested parties in its affairs. A failure to sustain such a coalition is likely to leave universities vulnerable to changes in political sentiment as public policies veer from one expenditure option to another in search of political advantage.

In establishing a learning market to vitalize a learning society, it is necessary to bear in mind two other considerations. To begin with, some of the changes that have been introduced into the public service more widely during the past 15 years may have useful lessons for higher education, particularly those which deal with increasing access to services, improving diversity in service provision and the creation of 'internal markets' and quasi-markets. The latter have emerged as realistic alternatives to both bureaucratic modes of service provision and fully privatized market systems.

Their essential characteristic is that public goods and services remain publicly funded but are provided by a variety of independent for-profit and non-profit organizations. Public funding can take place on the basis of contracts, vouchers or a formula-funded capitation system. Private funding can be deployed alongside public investment to allow individuals choices where different types of services are required. The shift from *mass* to *customized* production and consumption is driving changes as readily in the service sector as in manufacture, and this is likely to affect higher education too.

Giving an account of changes to universities in these terms may be one way of informing our understanding of the likely direction in which our institutions may need to evolve hereafter. This is likely to involve a change in the way universities conceive of themselves – from professional communities defined largely by academic judgements towards stakeholder communities defined by the needs of interested parties, including service users. This may be reflected in the rise of consumer sovereignty and, more troublesome for professionalized communities, the ascendancy of management as proxy for consumer interests.

But there is a second and more cautionary consideration. The operation of a 'learning market' does not guarantee a flawless transition to a fair and effective system of post-secondary and higher education. Indeed, left to itself, a learning market is capable of implosion and internal disintegration (intellectually as well as financially). Individuals can become lost in a morass of choices: choice itself can be restricted to options which command a premium in the market place; and market failure can lead to embarrassing gaps in the comprehensive coverage of higher education. Therefore, it is essential to understand the operation of the learning market *only* in the context of a learning society: it is the former which introduces the dynamics of change, while the latter bestows an encompassing legitimacy for the distribution of access, learning opportunities and outputs of the market. In this manner, the interaction of government policy and market relationships can be used to introduce profound changes into services, including higher education, which may otherwise be resistant to modernizing initiatives.

Building coalitions of support

Having set out the case, this discussion does not add voice to those who claim that everything we cherish in university life is now threatened; that our best efforts are being undermined; and that our qualities are undervalued by a public rendered insensitive by the assault on public services over the past two decades. Academics are notoriously adept at rattling their chains; every period of change appears to represent a new crisis; each age, a new decline. Student learning opportunities have increased and many more individuals are able to celebrate educational achievement at the highest level. The labour market has access to better qualified employees than ever before. And rising parental aspirations are likely to ensure that there is no reversal in the rate at which young people, and others, are able to move through university in the future. In so many ways, the next century is likely to be the age of higher education in the way that the present century became the age of schools.

One must also be careful not to 'blame the victim'. There is a genuine sense of grief, akin to bereavement, throughout the academic community as colleagues come to terms with loss of control and authority in their professional affairs. The rise of a 'new' managerialism has displaced professional

Table 5.1   Sectoral student : staff ratios

Ratios	1989–90 (actual %)	1992–3 (actual %)	1995–6 (estimate %)
Up to 10 : 1	17	16	15
Between 10 : 1 and 15 : 1	64	29	20
Between 15 : 1 and 20 : 1	14	44	44
Above 20 : 1	–	9	18
Not stated	5	2	3

Source: National Audit Office (1994: 33).

voice just as the extension of expenditure constraints to higher education has displaced former comforts and professional autonomy. Within less than a generation, conditions and relationships have changed to such an extent that few working in universities believe that the quality of professional life has improved. The ability to do a decent job of academic work to high standard is now hedged around with the pressures of administration, the scramble for funds, squabbles over priorities and the persistent noise of officialdom. Job insecurity has become an important factor which now defines work in universities, as 'soft' money replaces 'hard' money as the basis for staff employment.

For example, institutional income from non-government sources increased from 19 per cent in 1982–3 to 31 per cent by 1988–9 (National Audit Office 1994) while the proportion of academic staff financed wholly from university funds declined from 80 per cent in 1979 to 63 per cent by 1990 (Johnes and Taylor 1990) as universities strove to increase their cost recovery from alternative funding sources. Moreover, as Table 5.1 indicates, student : staff ratios have risen dramatically in a relatively short period as expansion in students numbers has not been reflected in additional academic staff appointments. It is something of an understatement to suggest that these are not the ideal conditions in which to anticipate the gracious cooperation of academic colleagues in the pursuit of controversial changes.

Nevertheless, in an attempt to come to terms with these diverse developments, I want to offer a frank and self-critical assessment of the contemporary position of universities in the UK. If we engage in such a critique, perhaps we can discover the means by which universities will be able to command public affection and thereby to assemble sustainable coalitions of popular support. It is the absence of such popular coalitions which has weakened the standing of higher education in the policy community and allowed the sector to be deflected from redefining its modern purpose. To this end, I take as a starting point the forthright comment of one longstanding observer of UK higher education: 'British universities need to cultivate friends more widely in society – and chiefly by providing services to them. But that runs against the strongly held attitudes of some academics, for whom it is a betrayal of the mission of the university' (Trow 1991: 21).

What Trow proposes for colleagues in UK higher education is something he observes throughout the American system: a closing of the gap between universities and society; a readiness to respond to a multiplicity of individual demands; and a dynamism which allows the forces of market competition to produce the diversity which meets those demands. In short, Trow is advocating the creation of strategic alliances for UK institutions by encouraging their repositioning from private cultural space into the public political domain. The effect would be to end the isolation of the academic community from the wider society and to accept a commitment to social inclusion and social justice as the defining purpose of the modern university. If this runs against the grain of academic life in the UK, as Trow suspects, then our higher education system may indeed be in crisis.

Avoiding the crisis, however, will require nothing less than a second reinvention of universities. The first followed nineteenth-century industrialization – a shift from theocratic to meritocratic dominance – in which the UK universities were supported as efficient agents for generating the ruling elite of the secular industrial state. The second repositioning will require a shift from meritocratic to democratic practice in which the academic community will need to be placed at the service of its 'customers' or service users: students, employers, global and local clients, as well as the state itself. In this second repositioning, UK higher education may need to by-pass 'mass' higher education in every respect except volume participation and move straight to 'customized' higher education: multiply diverse, technologically imaginative and flexible in the way learning, credentials and research outcomes are made available to different groups.

If, as I believe, universities are capable of reinventing themselves, then we do face the prospect of securing for higher education a place at the apex of public affairs, anchored in the lives and affections of millions of citizens and uncontestably connected to national economic success. To arrive at this intoxicating and unfamiliar state of affairs, universities may need to adopt a less defensive, more open-minded, self-critical and inventive stance than has hitherto been the case.

The end of political deference towards higher education?

How might we proceed? To begin with, changes to higher education over the past two decades or so are already producing a significant repositioning of universities in the United Kingdom. As I suggested at the beginning of this analysis, the ancient and generous bargain between universities and the state – effectively 'public funding on demand' – is being supplanted by an altogether more austere concordat. Public investment is giving way to private cash; public accountability is replacing professional trust. Conditions of sheltered privilege are being overtaken by the public obligations of modern society. Universities are expected no longer to supply education merely to an imperial elite; a broader version of higher education must now cater for a range of communities and negotiate the competing needs of each.

Moreover, universities in the UK and more widely are having to confront a greater degree of public interrogation of the quality, accessibility and rates of return to higher education. This may be seen as the outcome of a culture which now encourages individuals to expect access to higher education, but also to discriminate more readily on the basis of product, price, quality and reputation when making investment decisions. Although discernment of this character remains underdeveloped in the UK, it is only a matter of time before individuals generally begin to ask searching questions about the type of service they expect to receive from higher education providers. The banalities of current versions of 'student charters' and the paradisean images of recruitment prospectuses are unlikely to survive the more insistent demands of individuals who have incurred substantial private costs in seeking an appropriate learning programme in higher education.

Adding to the frustration of those who work in the sector, public concern over service quality and cost is matched only by public indifference to the special pleading of academics. If the basis of professional life has been eroded by expenditure constraints, as many academics maintain, then in the public mind this lies a considerable distance from the more immediate sympathies which are aroused by cuts to the health service, schools, transport systems and local government services. Universities are trapped between self-regarding anticipations of applause (for having expanded under trying conditions) and the hiss of escaping public confidence (as questions are raised about standards, employment prospects and the genuine commitment of universities to social justice). Despite the ample opportunities now available to prospective students, and despite the fact that more than one and a half million citizens makes up a powerful constituency of potential support, universities in the UK remain exceptionally vulnerable to criticism from government and to indifference from the public at large.

In short, a deference which has sustained the comforts and autonomy of institutions for centuries is giving way to the clamour and impatience of a politicized market place. Higher education has become just another service scrambling for a share of public and individual investment and, in the UK at least, it is not that comfortably positioned for this. Recent budgetary decisions make the point.

Financial displacement and the absence of public interest

In its 1995 public expenditure settlement, the UK Treasury deducted approximately £300 million from the budgets of British universities, trimming up to 12 per cent from revenue and capital spending over three years. This

Table 5.2   Higher education: unit public funding (1979 = 100; 1989 = rebased)

	1979	1981	1983	1985	1987	1990	1993	1995	1997	1999
Universities	100	101	104	101	100	98				
Polytechnics	100	96	92	85	83	79				
Joint						100	85	78	70	64

Source: Estimated from government expenditure plans 1979–98.

followed the imposition by the Higher Education Funding Councils three years earlier of annual 'efficiency gains' of between 1 and 3 per cent. Moreover, institutional capacity to accelerate out of the impending cash crisis by expanding participation had already been strictly circumscribed since 1992 by limits to overall full-time student numbers, a Treasury-led restriction intended to reduce the obligation of the state to fund student maintenance. It is a fair measure of the scale of the expenditure reductions to note that, some time in 1998, institutions of higher education in the United Kingdom will be teaching twice the number of students at almost half the price compared with levels of participation and expenditure in 1981.

Taking the extreme points on the curves of increased expansion and reduced expenditure over the decade 1989–98, participation in higher education will have expanded by 40 per cent but cash to universities will have increased by merely 4 per cent. Table 5.2 shows the extent of the decline in the unit of public funding, a decline even steeper than indicated here if the former polytechnics are treated separately. The effect is that for the first time in nearly a generation, the real cash value of the unit of funding will have fallen by 1998.

Although undoubtedly severe, this decline forms part of a sustained effort by government over a decade and a half to reduce significantly the level of expenditure on UK public services. To that end, government has pursued double-headed but possibly contradictory measures, increasing and decreasing competitive pressure within the higher education sector.

In the first place, the Treasury has sought public expenditure savings and increased efficiency directly through competitive pressure. The 'regulators', in the form of the funding councils, have acted as a proxy for a competitive market by seeking to squeeze out inefficiencies from monopoly providers by imposing 'efficiency' targets. On the other hand, as monopoly purchasers of full-time student places, the funding councils have also enabled government to ration the supply of places and determine the price at which it will fund them. This may have reduced public expenditure, but the policy has been anti-competitive to the extent that universities have been able to supply places well below current rates of demand. The effect has been to reduce the inclination of universities to innovate or diversify themselves in response to pressure from the recruitment market and to concentrate instead on defending their existing arrangements from further expenditure erosion.

At the same time, universities have been expected to manage attenuated resources with no loss of quality or effectiveness. Government has sought to sever the connection between the level of funding and the maintenance of quality by asserting the need for better service management and pointing to the persistently high rates of achievement among graduating students. In this respect at least, universities have been treated no differently from the Civil Service, local government, the health service, schools and colleges. Indeed, it might be argued that higher education leaders have been slow to recognize the run of the tide in other parts of the public sector and should not be surprised by subsequent developments. As Williams commented on an earlier occasion:

> [In 1969] Britain was one of the few industrially advanced countries that was still attempting to enter an age of mass higher education with academic assumptions and costs that were appropriate for a system with much more restricted access. It was more than a decade and several rounds of expenditure cuts later that this rather obvious truth began to sink home to leaders of university opinion.
>
> (Williams 1988: 61)

Yet neither the successful expansion of the sector over the past decade nor the expenditure crisis now confronting institutions appear to have aroused appropriate levels of public acclaim or, when the occasion demands it, public outcry. This indifference is intellectually surprising and politically alarming when one considers that higher education spends over £5 billion of public taxation and a further £2 billion of private sector cash, and provides learning opportunities for nearly two million citizens annually.

In early 1996, in a desperate attempt to attract public attention, the UK vice chancellors did propose to overcome the budgetary measures by imposing a sector-wide levy of £300 on new university entrants. For a few days, newspaper headlines did reflect public disquiet on the state of university finances, but thereafter the sector was left with the residue: an ambiguous reaction by students and the academic community to proposals from highly paid vice chancellors for an individual levy, and then a rejection of the proposal by the vice chancellors' committee itself. For observers outside the sector, the entire episode appeared to be a strange way of building a multipartite coalition to support investment in higher education, and the consequences may revisit universities in the future.

Repositioning within the policy community

For public policy-makers, higher education is seen as too isolated from economic needs and too insular socially. It is seen as being constituted by self-serving academic oligarchies producing students ill-equipped either for employment or for further research. At worst, its 'lumbering obsolescence' is perceived to consume rather than produce energy and momentum; to consume public expenditure rather than produce socially necessary goods. As *The Economist* has noted, assent to university claims for a place high on the public spending agenda cannot be assumed:

> During the fat years after 1945 someone was always there to pick up the bill. Universities were seen by right-wing governments as engines of economic growth, by left-wing governments as agents of social equality, and by taxpayers as avenues of social mobility. No longer. Politicians and parents are scrutinising the bill and even refusing to pay. Every-where politicians on left and right are wondering whether the State ought to be sinking such huge sums into higher education.
>
> (*Economist*, December 1993: 55)

This process is by no means confined to the United Kingdom. Throughout the United States, popular support for higher education is under strain. The escalating costs of tuition have outstripped federal aid compensations leaving both the wealthy and the poor at the mercy of rising costs. Universities, particularly those in the public sector, such as the State University of New York or the universities of the California State system, now face a fiscal crisis of substantial magnitude: cost-cutting boards of trustees, the rolling back of public access programmes. In Australia and across much of Western Europe also, the demands of economic and organizational restructuring have produced a reduced confidence in the capacity of the university to deliver its promises of economic growth, social justice, personal advance-ment and intellectual renewal. For emerging nations that might look to universities as an engine of cultural modernization and economic vitaliza-tion, the costs to individual and state of investing in higher education can be crippling, particularly where student subsidy costs undermine wage lev-els in the labour market (World Bank 1994).

This is not to suggest that UK higher education has failed to command the attention of the policy community. Over the past ten years, the sector has been aggressively raked over like no other segment of the education service, with the possible exception of the 16–19 qualifications structure (see, for example and comparison, Richardson *et al.* 1993: 34–7).

Numerous reports have been written by various national bodies on the need to reform higher education, to expand provision, for better employ-ment relevance, to shift from the same type of education albeit for more students to a new type of higher education better suited to national priori-ties at the start of a new millennium. These have included two White Papers (DES 1987, 1991), one National Commission on Education report (1993), a Commission on Social Justice report (1994) and latterly various reports and consultative papers on cultural change in universities (Ball 1990; Duke 1992; Finegold *et al.* 1992); employer preferences (CBI 1994; Association of Graduate Recruiters 1993, 1995); technologies for teaching and learn-ing (MacFarlane 1992); the impact of adult participation (NIACE 1993); student choice, credential mobility, quality and funding in the learning market (Robertson 1994); lifetime learning and higher education (Coffield

1995; DfEE 1995); competitiveness reports from the DTI (1994–6); the changing prospects for UK higher education in the UK (Williams and Fry 1994; Schuller 1995); and international comparisons (OECD 1993, 1996; World Bank 1994; UNESCO 1995).

A government review of the sector was commissioned towards the end of 1994 in an effort to pull together some of this work, but by 1996 this had merged into the Dearing Review. As I mentioned earlier, decisions on the future direction of higher education offer so few guarantees of electoral advantage to policy-makers that there has been bipartisan agreement to shuffle off proposals beyond a general election.

From 'elite' to 'crowded' higher education

Universities are being tested by unusual and formidable forces. As modern economies restructure and reposition themselves in a competitive, post-imperial and global market place, governments require that higher education provides democratic access to high-quality credentials for greater numbers of students, unmatched by commensurate resources, while at the same time demonstrating that they are contributing directly to national economic effectiveness through the production of relevant new knowledge and highly qualified output. The expectations of universities have rarely been more varied. As Burton Clark (1993: 263) has observed: 'With each passing decade a modern or modernising system of higher education is expected and inspired to do more for other portions of society, from strengthening the economy and invigorating government to developing individual talents and personalities and aiding the pursuit of happiness.' In the UK, but also more widely, 'aiding the pursuit of happiness' has been put on hold for the time being. Universities must now maintain standards despite attenuated resources; educate a more diverse range of students; introduce more flexible curricula, including new forms of learning delivery and assessment; teach and research more intensively; prepare students for employment more effectively; contribute to improved economic competitiveness and to local economic success; and replace public investment with the merchant's penny whenever they are able.

On the other hand, in what should be a basis for celebration but is as often a source of despair, there are now twice the number of institutions able to call themselves 'university', a threefold increase in participation rates and a doubling of institutional size by student numbers in little over a decade. By these measures the UK easily meets the conditions of a 'mass' system of higher education (Trow 1981, 1993). There are now more students enrolled with the Open University, or following higher education courses in further education colleges, than there were in the entire university system in 1963 at the time of the Robbins Report. Today, with over 1.5 million students attending higher education courses, it has become something of a commonplace, verging on complacency, to argue that we have passed into a 'mass' system.

At the same time, in ways which are currently less easy to quantify, three times the number of graduates will be leaving universities to seek jobs in a changing and unfamiliar labour market. 'Generation X' and its honorary adult members are being faced with a 'downsizing' labour market, in which thousands of traditional graduate jobs, and potentially hundreds of thousands of graduate careers, have changed or disappeared.

In the earlier sheltered system, a close alignment between the learning market and the labour market was achieved by rationing. A restricted supply of places in higher education ensured that the high professions and large corporations could always recruit for senior positions from a carefully prepared cadre of qualified employees. But when other countries were expanding their higher education systems after 1950 in response to the needs of mass production economies, the UK continued for decades with its policy of rationing.

By the time the UK caught up, in the later 1980s, the global economy had moved on again. Large companies no longer expect to mass-recruit graduates and, in the UK at least, the rapidly expanding smaller company sector has not traditionally looked to the graduate market for employees. Where they try, smaller firms and larger companies also find that potential recruits lack the flexibility and resourcefulness they seek (CBI 1994; Association of Graduate Recruiters 1995).

For forthcoming generations of graduates, newly enfranchised by credentials and seeking sustainable employment, the UK may have expanded an obsolete style of higher education, and too late (see Murphy 1993, for example). We may be in danger of producing larger numbers of graduates who are no longer suitably qualified for the new labour market. The overproduction of graduates from an 'elite' system is therefore no substitute, in terms of national effectiveness or social justice, for the derationed production of graduates from a modernized and reformed learning market. Yet closer inspection suggests that, as a consequence of transition perhaps, the system is simply 'crowded' – values and structures have been slower to change than rates of participation.

Accordingly, higher education is experiencing a series of displacements and relocations which are disturbing longstanding relationships between universities and the wider society. For Scott (1995) this process is the working through of profound changes in the intellectual condition of (post)modern society: a flight from certainty, a loss of intimacy, a challenge to intellectual authority and expertise. Others have described the changes in more material terms: a shift in the balance of power from institutional autonomy towards the state and 'state bureaucrats' (Russell 1993; Salter and Tapper 1994; Miller 1995), or towards managerialist demands for surveillance and control (Barnett 1994). The effect appears to be the same: loss of professional voice, an undermining of the academic mandate, a degradation of professional status, a 'decline in donnish dominion' (Halsey 1992).

In the context of public services generally, higher education is being displaced as an educational segment different from all others. In terms of public policy discussions and public expenditure decisions, higher education is being seen merely as the latest stage in the learning careers of individuals, closely connected to the promotion of lifetime learning initiatives and less clearly defined by social exclusiveness or special consideration. Indeed, higher education has for the time being lost the ability to protect its public resource base and has come under increasing scrutiny in terms of value for money. Public policy attention has turned to the greater social rates of return to be achieved from investment in pre-school education (National Commission on Education 1993; Commission on Social Justice 1994), or to the affordable opportunities that can be created in the more biddable post-secondary and further education colleges. In this regard, universities have arranged themselves on the battlefield of public policy as an academic equivalent of the Maginot Line – impossible to breach but easy to circumvent.

Furthermore, higher education is being displaced as a sphere of public activity accountable principally to itself. The encroachment of the state has been inexorable over the past 30 years but it has been eased by the absence of any significant recognition among universities themselves that they might be subject to initiatives for greater accountability. Throughout the 1980s, as other public services were expected to demonstrate value for money and services were cut back, many universities continued as if nothing could change for them – an unsustainable other-worldliness. As Shattock has noted in the context of the University Grants Committee's (UGC's) reliance on a block-grant funding mechanism:

> [this lay] at the root of the universities' reluctance to innovate because the block grant offered no incentive for change. Since the reward structures did not encourage it, it was only too easy for universities to resist new ideas out of a fear of stepping outside the established pattern of activity. *Since the UGC did not monitor how its resources were spent,* it encouraged a degree of cosiness and complacency in universities which meant that they were quite unprepared for the Thatcher revolution.
>
> (Shattock 1994: 145; emphasis added)

The failure to monitor the spending of resources was entirely in keeping with the 'old bargain'. Universities were allocated public money and how they spent it was largely a matter for individual institutions. High quality was assumed and the state did not enquire too closely about what it was paying for, a practice which endorsed a rather lazy interpretation of academic autonomy. Although the UGC funding model was admired by university professionals throughout the world as an 'eighth wonder', it was in fact a small miracle, utterly inimitable by any state which sought responsible financial management.

From the 1980s onwards, this proved to be the case for the UK as well.

The 'new bargain' tied universities much more closely to an internal quasi-market in which purchaser–provider relationships have led to the development of contractual arrangements between the state and institutions. In this context, contract compliance has become the means by which the monopoly state purchaser has ensured that 'product' targets are met by institutional providers (course recruitment and so forth) to an acceptable quality threshold (for example, via quality assessment arrangements).

Emerging policy agendas: elements in the new bargain

If the picture were not sufficiently sobering, universities must now confront five longer-term challenges to their identity, each a policy option under active discussion. First, developments in technology are rapidly permitting new forms of information management and presentation. The emergence of integrated, interactive and customized information platforms will soon consolidate the impact of the current generation of computers, enabling individuals to access and manipulate sources of information and learning support beyond the means conventionally available in the university. This has led Hague (1991), for example, to argue that technological initiatives of this nature will lead to the decomposition of the traditional university and its replacement in the form of customized access to international sources of information via the Internet or similar systems. More restrained but equally far-reaching proposals have emerged from the MacFarlane Report (MacFarlane 1992), which seek to encourage the adoption of new learning technologies as a means of reducing the unit costs of learning to the individual and eventually to the state.

Second, new forms of knowledge production in centres outside the university – in commercial laboratories, government research centres, 'think tanks' and consultancies – are beginning to raise questions about the sustainability of the hegemony which universities have enjoyed for centuries over the production of advanced knowledge (see Gibbons *et al.* 1994). In some ways, how universities arrange their affairs and delineate the boundaries of knowledge look increasingly out of step in a world seeking solutions to trans-disciplinary problems. The shift in the locus of knowledge production, defined by Gibbons as a move from 'mode 1' to 'mode 2' knowledge and outlined by Coffield (this volume), reflects a decline in the supremacy of knowledge defined by the judgements of academic *producers* and a rise in socio-commercial interests which define knowledge in terms of its application and utility for knowledge *consumers*.

Taken together, accelerating innovations in information technology and the rise of new sources of knowledge production are likely to produce a third challenge in the form of new entrants to the learning market in higher education. For competitors to enter the market, it would take nothing other than a government-inspired requirement for universities to be accredited only when they meet certain standards of performance. This would circumvent the need to develop 'new' (probably private) universities in the image of the old, since such 'universities' would already exist in the commercial sector. Others would emerge from the further education colleges. Their accreditation, where they meet approved performance standards, could effectively remove from universities their one defining monopoly characteristic: control over the award of their own degree qualifications. New market entrants could be granted similar powers where they meet the required standards, unleashing hitherto unrealized competitive pressures and producing a plausible and arguably popular de-monopolization of higher education. Competitors could pick off market segments (i.e. those for whom 'campus' life is not attractive or relevant, and who have no institutional loyalty). Under these conditions, universities would find themselves squeezed by further education colleges in their local markets and displaced by multinational firms in parts of their national and international markets.

Fourth, universities face the prospect of diminished expectations. Decoupled from growth in a competitive market place, as economies look elsewhere for new ideas and forms of competitive advantage beyond human capital, universities are being set on the defensive in their search for an unambiguously necessary and socially useful role. To date, it has become conventional to assume that universities will be protected against adverse policies by the need for economies to produce high levels of knowledge-rich labour (Reich 1991) and by the assumption that the growth sectors in the labour market favour highly qualified labour (Rajan 1992). Moreover, the skills of a workforce cannot so easily be exported and therefore nations which produce highly qualified labour protect themselves with an enduring competitive advantage.

This remains true for as long as the labour market continues to seek 'oven-ready' labour fresh from university at any early age. But conventional patterns of recruitment may already be breaking down. The structure of the labour market is changing rapidly (see, for example, Penn *et al.* 1994; Rubery and Wilkinson 1994; Crompton *et al.* 1996). In 1990 large companies recruited 80 per cent of graduates available for work; in 1995 this had declined to 50 per cent. Small and medium-sized enterprises (SMEs) are the areas of swiftest growth in jobs, but in the UK they do not tend to employ graduates. The high cost and risk of failure, the unrealistic expectations and poor adaptability of graduates militate against their attractiveness for small-sized employers, who need immediate added value and cannot afford development programmes. Either SMEs will come to value conventional university outputs as graduates begin to saturate the labour market, or universities will need to qualify far more versatile and resourceful graduates and other qualified candidates.

Moreover, Brown and Scase (1994) make the point that new, more personalized, recruitment practices may act against meritocratic job selection by favouring those individual qualities which are only assessable by subjective measures and are more frequently observed among candidates from specific social backgrounds. Thus the shift from explicit to implicit selection criteria, and the emphasis on 'social skills' or 'team-working', for example, allow employers to select 'people we know' from 'universities we trust' rather than on the basis of credential performance alone. The effect is to emphasize particular forms of cultural capital and provide a means by which the educated middle class can protect their positional advantage in the labour market, sheltering themselves from competitive credential pressure (see also Brown 1995; Brown and Lauder 1996). This analysis cuts across more optimistic assessments of the consequences for learners and national economies of credential achievement and mobility (Robertson 1996) and may well require universities to engage in a fundamental examination of their responsibilities to students seeking entry to labour markets. Put precisely, universities may need to switch their priorities from investment in 'entrance' to investment in 'exit' if they are to equip students adequately for employment. If they fail to do this, universities may find that competitors elsewhere in the learning market – institutes and colleges pledged to deliver occupational standards, for example – will provide this service to students.

Fifth, higher education is being faced with the challenge of customization. If one combines the policy initiative above – the impact of information technology on learning delivery, the development of application-based knowledge, the increase in educational providers and new market entrants, and the personalization of recruitment to the labour market – it should not take long before one realizes that the individualization of positional advantage is likely to be reflected in the demands learners will make on their programmes of study.

Developments in providing for genuine flexibility and choice in learning programmes have been steady but slow (Robertson 1994). The rhetoric of modularization, credit accumulation and transfer, and work-based learning, for example, has been impressive, but closer inspection suggests that fundamental change has yet to be achieved. Students enjoy some modest flexibility within programmes but there is little inter-institutional credit transfer (Robertson 1996). Furthermore, internal market transactions are circumscribed by funding and regulatory restrictions on personal mobility; while inter-segmental mobility (between further and higher education, for example) has been affected by policy changes restricting the growth in student numbers.

Nevertheless, those aspects of higher education culture which imply that the quality of the learning experience is defined by the discipline and the course may be displaced in decades to come by a much more opportunistic treatment of higher education by students. In this respect, their 'opportunism' is likely to be a reflection of a need to respond to scarcity signals in the labour market more quickly than institutions are able to redesign their courses. Therefore, institutions and other providers which can supply customization of the learning experience – varying the style, content, technology and cost of learning – may secure for themselves an important advantage in the learning market.

Towards a modernized and reformed higher education

What can be said about the principles which need to define the 'new' bargain for higher education? First, as I have already implied, universities should become the leading institutions of a learning society – leading not simply through their excellence and exclusivity, but through the inspiration they provide for the democratic mass of society. They should be responsible for the creation of a sustainable culture of aspiration which encourages most people to anticipate some experience of higher education at some point in their lives.

This may not be welcomed by those, in universities and beyond, who believe that one purpose of education is to prepare people for a place in a predetermined social and economic hierarchy. If we continue to foster that view in the UK, then our universities are likely to remain little more than centres for the cultural reinforcement of a selective and socially privileged segment of the population, causing us to fall further behind other countries in the effective exploitation of national potential.

Second, to avoid this state of affairs, universities could do well to consider themselves more like public services of the modern period (Ranson and Stewart 1994). Public services are generally democratically accessible to the extent that their principal obligation is to offer a service to whoever needs it, restricting access only because of limited resources. On all other occasions, access to public services is made available in a fair and impartial manner according to rational and publicly negotiated criteria. When public services operate according to 'private' rules, their probity is called into question, as might be the case in the allocation of public housing, Civil Service or local authority jobs and so forth. Yet an enduring feature of university life has been the existence of private rules, reinforced from time to time by the state's acceptance that institutions can be left to determine their own affairs.

The apparent sovereignty of higher education institutions works well when matters of academic freedom are at stake, but private rules work against the public interest on three grounds: first, when universities deploy public resources according to their own priorities and contrary to the national interest; second, when universities impose rules which imply preference for particular social groups; and third, when universities conspire against their own members. As pressure has mounted on universities to define themselves as 'managed businesses' in the image of commercial organizations, so the existence of private rules is beginning to collide with the general public good.

Third, to counter any tendency towards autocracy and offence to the public good, universities may need to establish a powerful sense of internal citizenship – an internal bargain with members of the academic and wider professional community, as well as students – in order to rebalance the relationship between management and other groups in the academic community. A central feature of modern public services has been the displacement of professional judgements by management action. This has been one of the least successful aspects of the transformation and, in the case of universities, materially disturbs the capacity for inventive and dissentful inquiry. The losses to efficiency and quality may take some time to come through but it is quite clear that the employment practices of a university, the way it treats its staff, have a quantifiable impact on its reputation and therefore on its effectiveness. Well nurtured staff respond well in organizations which depend for their vitality on a commitment to public service values. Brutalized and unfairly treated professional staff simply walk away; those who cannot, find other sources of comfort.

If universities were to establish meaningful 'good employer' charters alongside their 'student charters', this might go some way to establishing rights for 'internal citizens'. If not, we are likely to witness a further polarization of the academic community into those who enjoy tenure but are otherwise disaffected with management hegemony, and others who have never enjoyed tenure, and who remain threatened by prospects of insecure employment and loss of professional voice. In either case, the consequences for higher education will be poor if internal citizens do not receive a mandate to participate fully in their academic communities.

Of course, a concept of 'internal citizenship' may require some redefinition of the meaning of 'academic community' and 'academic autonomy', yielding new forms of public accountability and legitimation. The following dimensions might be considered in determining this aspect of the 'new' bargain: an acceptance of some external scrutiny and critique of the practices and outputs of higher education; the introduction of more democratic and responsible forms of institutional governance, including the replacement of quangoid governing machinery by more open and renewable bodies reflecting the full range of stakeholders; the separation of individual academic freedom (i.e. the right of individual academics to think, write and express themselves without fear of retribution) from institutional academic autonomy (i.e. the right of the university to define its purpose and practices as it chooses). The first should be enshrined in law, if necessary; the second seems to be negotiable, at least to the extent that the state must reserve unto itself the right to judge whether higher education is performing to the greater benefit of the public good in direct proportion to the investment it makes in the service.

A 'new' bargain between learners and institution

Finally, if universities are to see themselves as institutions in the public service, they may need fundamentally to redefine their relationship with learners. I have already spoken of the prospects for the customization of learning in decades to come; this needs to be taken to its logical conclusion. To date, students have been keen to obtain a place in higher education and this has guaranteed a premium return in employment prospects. Since the supply of places in UK higher education has substantially failed to meet rising levels of demand across the range of courses, universities have had no great incentive to respond to the individual needs of students. In the present period of retrenchment, this source of competitive pressure has fallen away completely, and it seems likely that universities may return to familiar patterns of provision. Students will then bear the burden of competing for relatively scarce places and, if the past is a guide, will simply decline to compete. Application rates will fall and policy-makers will assume that demand has tailed off too.

If we are to reach a 'new' bargain for higher education in the twenty-first century, one condition must be that students will not have to rely on the goodwill of the state to supply places. In one sense, students do not rely on this now – they can 'purchase' their higher education from the learning market. Many do, by joining the Open University or other part-time programmes, where they pay a price to be denied access to the full range of learning resources available to full-time students who obtain their higher education relatively free from personal cost. Although this inequality is rapidly changing as full-time students meet new obligations to contribute to their maintenance, the abiding relationship is one where students bear the responsibilities for paying for higher education, but receive few rights over the character or quality of the product they purchase. Instead, institutional managers or the agencies of the state – funding councils, for example – act as proxy for the interests of the student-consumer, a largely unsatisfactory state of affairs.

The advantage to universities in promoting a purchaser–provider relationship with students themselves is that an alliance of higher education and its users, based on mutually advantageous transactions, would be one sure means of securing for the longer term a stake in the affections of the wider public. This would require universities to accept that student choice does not end with the selection of university and course – that was the 'old' provider-led bargain. In the 'new' bargain, students might expect a much greater degree of flexibility over the pace, shape and content of learning. Although this inevitably raises issues of quality and standards in the minds of universities and policy-makers alike, the trade-off for universities lies in the formation of alliances with the broad mass of students based on the satisfaction of need.

I have suggested on other occasions (for example, Robertson 1994, 1995) that I believe that certain aspects of the reform of UK public services have improved prospects for social justice. This includes both the extension of choice to consumers and the means to exercise choice in the service market. To this end, the idea of a 'voucher' to supply students with genuine financial leverage cannot be ruled out as a suitable means of consolidating a 'new' bargain between providers and learners.

Conclusion: social justice in a learning market

This raises the principal question: can social justice be achieved within a learning market? The problem with markets is that, unmodified, they confirm inequalities (Ranson 1994). Markets 'fail' when particular groups are denied access to socially desirable 'products' – in this case, higher qualifications. But government action can also 'fail' to deliver fair access to social benefits. The question we must resolve in the 'new' bargain for higher education is whether to rely on improved government action for social justice in the learning market, or whether to deploy government action at points where the market fails (Levačić 1991).

To date, large numbers of prospective learners have not been able to rely on government action; they have needed to purchase their learning opportunities from the learning market. Would it be worse if every learner seeking the benefits which higher education bestows were obliged to trade in the learning market? It could not yield more inequality than the current arrangements and, with appropriate government intervention, it could yield far less. The prospect of establishing for learners a basic entitlement to trade in the learning market – a 'learning voucher' – could be the means by which providers begin to form new alliances with social groups, with their local and regional communities and with employer partners. If the 'voucher' were an entitlement, and if it were coupled with an aid strategy to support the financially dispossessed, far more individuals would seek a place in university. Institutions would then be under greater competitive pressure to respond to the needs of students, potentially cementing long-lasting alliances of mutual gain.

The 'new' bargain which universities seek may be formed out of the 'old' bargain. The Dearing Committee may well stay within the carefully circumscribed boundaries of the politically deliverable, preferring less radical solutions to funding higher education which have the effect of burdening students but denying them the rights of internal citizens. If we are to strike out for a genuine 'new' bargain for a new century, then more radical ideas may well need to be explored; among these, a connection between social justice and the learning market might well provide the relationship we seek.

References

Association of Graduate Recruiters (1993) *Roles for Graduates in the 21st Century.* London, AGR.

Association of Graduate Recruiters (1995) *Skills for Graduates in the 21st Century.* London, AGR.

Ball, Sir Christopher (1990) *More Means Different: Widening Access to Higher Education.* London, Royal Society of Arts.

Barnett, R. (1994) *The Limits to Competence.* Buckingham, Open University Press/ SRHE.

Brown, P. (1995) Cultural capital and social exclusion: some observations on recent trends in education, employment and the labour market, *Work, Employment & Society*, 9(1), 29–51.

Brown, P. and Lauder, H. (1996) Education, globalisation and economic development, *Journal of Education Policy*, 11(1), 1–25.

Brown, P. and Scase, R. (1994) *Higher Education and Corporate Realities*. London, UCL Press.

CBI (1994) *Thinking Ahead: Ensuring the Expansion of Higher Education into the 21st Century*. London, Confederation of British Industry.

Clark, B. R. (1993) The problem of complexity in modern higher education, in S. Rothblatt and B. Wittrock (eds) *The European and American University since 1800*. Cambridge, Cambridge University Press.

Coffield, F. (ed.) (1995) *Higher Education in a Learning Society*. Durham, University of Durham School of Education (report of the symposium, St Edmund Hall, Oxford).

Commission on Social Justice (1994) *Social Justice: Strategies for National Renewal*. London, Vintage.

Crompton, R., Gaille, D. and Purcell, K. (eds) (1996) *Changing Forms of Employment*. London, Routledge.

DES (1987) *Higher Education: Meeting the Challenge*. Cmnd 114. London, HMSO.

DES (1991) *Higher Education: a New Framework*. Cmnd 1541. London, HMSO.

DfEE (1995) *Lifetime Learning: a Consultation Document*. London, DfEE.

Duke, C. (1992) *The Learning University*. Buckingham, Open University Press/SRHE.

DTI (1994) *Competitiveness: Helping Business to Win*. Cmnd 2563. London, HMSO.

DTI (1995) *Competitiveness: Forging Ahead*. Cmnd 2867. London, HMSO.

DTI (1996) *Competitiveness: Creating the Enterprise Centre of Europe*. Cmnd 3330. London, HMSO.

Economist (1993) Universities: towers of babble, 25 Dec. 1993–7 Jan. 1994, 54–6.

Finegold, D., Keep, E., Miliband, D., Robertson, D., Sisson, K. and Ziman, J. (1992) *Higher Education: Expansion and Reform*. London, IPPR.

Gibbons, M., Limonges, C., Nowotny, H., Schwartzman, S., Scott, P. and Trow, M. (1994) *The New Production of Knowledge: the Dynamics of Science and Research in Contemporary Societies*. London: Sage.

Hague, D. (1991) *Beyond Universities: a New Republic of the Intellect*. London, IEA.

Halsey, A. (1992) *The Decline of Donnish Dominion*. Oxford, Oxford University Press.

Johnes, J. and Taylor, J. (1990) *Performance Indicators in Higher Education*. Buckingham, Open University Press/SRHE.

Levačić, R. (1991) Markets and government: an overview, in G. Thompson *et al.* (eds) *Markets, Hierarchies and Networks*. London, Sage.

MacFarlane, A. (1992) *Teaching and Learning in an Expanding Higher Education System*. Edinburgh, Committee of Scottish University Principals.

Miller, H. D. R. (1995) *The Management of Change in Universities*. Buckingham, Open University Press/SRHE.

Murphy, J. (1993) A degree of waste: the economic benefits of educational expansion, *Oxford Review of Education*, 19(1), 9–31.

National Audit Office (1994) *The Financial Health of Higher Education Institutions in England*. HC 13. London, NAO.

National Commission on Education (1993) *Learning to Succeed*. London, NCE.

NIACE (1993) *An Adult Higher Education*. Leicester, NIACE.

OECD (1993) *Education at a Glance*. Paris, OECD.

OECD (1996) *Thematic Review of Tertiary Education: Progress Report.* Paris, OECD.

Penn, R., Rose, M. and Rubery, J. (eds) (1994) *Skill and Occupational Change.* Oxford, Oxford University Press.

Rajan, A. (1992) *1990s: Where Will the New Jobs Be?* London, Institute of Careers Guidance/CREATE.

Ranson, S. (1994) *Towards the Learning Society.* London, Cassell.

Ranson, S. and Stewart, J. (1994) *Management for the Public Domain.* London, Macmillan.

Reich, R. B. (1991) *The Work of Nations.* London, Simon & Schuster.

Richardson, W., Woolhouse, J. and Finegold, D. (eds) (1993) *The Reform of Post-16 Education and Training in England and Wales.* Harlow, Longman.

Robertson, D. (1994) *Choosing to Change – Extending Access, Choice and Mobility in Higher Education.* London, HEQC.

Robertson, D. (1995) The reform of higher education: for social equity, individual choice and mobility, in F. Coffield (ed.) *op. cit.*

Robertson, D. (1996) Credit transfer and the mobility of credentials in UK higher education: the evolution of policies, meanings and purposes, *Journal of Education Policy*, 11(1), 53–74.

Rubery, J. and Wilkinson, F. (eds) (1994) *Employer Strategy and the Labour Market.* Oxford, Oxford University Press.

Russell, C. (1993) *Academic Freedom.* London, Routledge.

Salter, B. and Tapper, T. (1994) *The State and Higher Education.* Ilford, Woburn Press.

Schuller, T. (ed.) (1995) *The Changing University?* Buckingham, Open University Press/SRHE.

Scott, P. (1995) *The Meanings of Mass Higher Education.* Buckingham, Open University Press/SRHE.

Shattock, M. (1994) *The UGC and the Management of British Universities.* Buckingham, Open University Press/SRHE.

Trow, M. (1981) Comparative perspectives on access, in O. Fulton (ed.) *Access to Higher Education.* Leverhulme Studies 2. Guildford, SRHE.

Trow, M. (1991) Comparative perspectives on policy, in R. Berdahl, G. Moodie and I. Spitzberg (eds) *Quality and Access in Higher Education.* Buckingham, Open University Press/SRHE.

Trow, M. (1993) Comparative perspectives on British and American higher education, in S. Rothblatt and B. Wittrock (eds) *The European and American University since 1800.* Cambridge, Cambridge University Press.

UNESCO (1995) *Policy Paper for Change and Development in Higher Education.* Paris, UNESCO.

Williams, G. (1988) The debate about funding mechanisms, *Oxford Review of Education*, 13(1), 59–68.

Williams, G. and Fry, H. (1994) *Long-term Prospects for Higher Education – a Report to the CVCP.* London, Institute of Education.

World Bank (1994) *Higher Education: the Lessons of Experience.* Washington, DC, World Bank.

6

Changing Frameworks and Qualifications

Stephen McNair

It is easy to be trapped in customary ways of seeing one's environment, and fail to see radical change approaching, or even to perceive it when it has happened. A caterpillar delivering a lecture on the future might talk about many things – plant growth, reproduction rates, air pollution, the prospect for bigger and better caterpillars. What it would be unlikely to discuss is butterflies!

The year 1990 was such a significant, but largely unnoticed, break point in the development of higher education in England and Wales. In that year NIACE published a policy paper, *Adults in Higher Education* (NIACE 1990), which sought to encourage higher education to take notice of its adult learners, who were seen as a neglected minority within a system dominated by 'traditional' learners. However, in 1990, for the first time, the number of mature students (i.e. over 21 at entry for undergraduates and over 25 at entry from postgraduates) admitted to higher education in Britain exceeded the number of 'traditional' ones, and the proportion has increased steadily since. Two years later, suspecting that we might have passed a significant milestone unnoticed, NIACE decided to review the new position, considering what an adult majority might mean for higher education, its purposes, methods and organization. The new document, *An Adult Higher Education*, was published in late 1993, followed by a national consultation. This chapter reflects on the issues which the document explored, and the issues which arose from the responses.

Most critically, it poses the dilemma at the heart of the debate: that we wish to expand access to higher education, while maintaining quality, reducing (or at least not increasing) public funding and retaining the honours degree as the benchmark of what higher education is. This equation does not add up, and if we do not wish to see quality and resourcing gradually eroded away, we have to consider which element can be sacrificed, or redefined, to make the equation balance. This chapter offers one possible solution to the dilemma: that we should restructure higher education qualifications into two distinct phases, funded in different ways. Not everyone will agree, and the solution which I sketch may be wrong, but if the formulation of the dilemma is right, we will need to seek alternative solutions: the status quo is not an option.

A changing world

Since we have to do this within the context of a rapidly changing world, and a rapidly changing higher education system, I wish to comment briefly on four aspects of change which have a particular relevance to higher education. In doing so, I should make it clear that I assume that the primary purpose of higher education is the creation, testing and transmission of knowledge in all its forms, and that it is unhelpful and unrealistic in considering this to draw crude distinctions between activities usually described as 'teaching', 'scholarship', 'research' and 'consultancy': all contribute to the broader purpose, and their interlock is much more complex than is generally recognized.

My first aspect of change is globalization, which raises both cultural and economic issues, of which the former are less often commented on in debates on higher education. The development of communication technologies in recent years offers us access to wider worlds, and challenges our ability to defend our own identities. As the experience of China and the Tiananmen Square events demonstrates, even the largest and most authoritarian state can no longer prevent its citizens from communicating with the world outside. Conversely, no one is protected from the footprint of the satellite broadcasters. The technologies bring with them value systems (democracy, individualism, market ideologies, nationalism etc.) which challenge our notions of who we are, and where the boundaries are around our own identity. Throughout the world one sees cultures brought into direct contact with others, with resulting conflicts and tensions, and old accommodations and boundaries tested by exposure to new worlds and values. And as we become citizens of a global society, too large for many of us to relate to, a countervailing pressure develops to redefine our identities in smaller communities – geographical, ethnic, religious, linguistic or national.

This presents a particular challenge to higher education, which has traditionally played a key role in understanding, interpreting and transmitting culture. Through the social sciences, higher education is one of the places where we study others, learning to understand the similarities and differences of others, while, through the arts and humanities, it is also one of the places where we define and transmit our own identities and values. At the same time, for those of us who participate in higher education, it is one of the places where we learn to be members of our own society, or at least of a particular class within it. Globalization makes these issues not for an esoteric minority of anthropologists, but for everyone.

A more widely discussed dimension of globalization is economic. Work migrates around the world with increasing ease. Once this involved only low-skill manual work, or the copying of ideas and products from the developed world by poor-quality imitators in Asia. Now it affects all of us. Professional work can be, and is being, exported to countries like India, with low wages and a surplus of graduate level skills, and electronic communications make such moves much easier. I do not need to know where the work is done as long as the results emerge from my computer terminal, linked to global networks which increasingly behave like financial markets, accountable to and understood fully by no one (no one 'manages' or controls the Internet, any more than anyone manages the stock market). Information, like money, can move freely around the world, to where it is used most 'efficiently', without any national or regional commitment.

The second aspect of change is in employment, and links closely to the globalization of work. Technology is changing the nature and distribution of work in fundamental ways. It makes it possible for individuals to produce more, more quickly and cheaply. It also makes it possible to individualize production. The development of personal computing is an obvious example: the individual private purchaser can choose between a great range of manufacturers, most of whom are willing, in addition to their standard range, to produce an individual machine, in which 20 or more components can be separately specified for no extra cost. The days when Henry Ford could offer cars in 'any colour as long as it's black' are long gone. The economies of mass production are no longer overwhelming, and no longer need to imply uniformity. In a similar way, computerized systems enable an engineering firm to create a prototype on its main production line by a temporary adjustment to the computer controls, where it previously had to maintain a separate plant. They also make it possible for much development and testing to be done in simulation, making testing more thorough, and providing more scope for creativity and innovation because it is possible to explore multiple solutions and hypotheses at minimal cost.

The results are complex and paradoxical. As Robert Reich has argued persuasively, the wealth of nations in the future will lie in their intellectual capacity, not in their supplies of raw materials or financial base (Reich 1991). Technology is improving the quality of products, the lives of consumers and the satisfaction of those who produce. The skill levels of those working in the new, more complex and flexible plant rise, while consumption of materials and levels of pollution decline. For those with high-level skills, they open new opportunities for creativity and personal satisfaction, not to mention profit. However, they require fewer people, and the effects for individuals and communities can be disastrous: there is a shrinking place for the low skilled, and the closure of redundant plant may remove the principal *raison d'être* of a whole community, with the attendant social and cultural upheaval. Reich has argued that these changes are creating a global class of 'symbolic analysts', who are the principal beneficiaries, and who are increasingly detached from any particular location, and from the rest of the population. Higher education is one of the principal tools for the creation and maintenance of such a class, and in carrying out this function it allocates social and economic benefits to individuals, as well as creating the base for a productive economy.

My third theme is knowledge. All the predictions are that the economy of the future will be driven by knowledge: the creation and application of new ideas, and the adaptation of old ones to new contexts. Those with the greatest rewards and satisfactions, on whom the economy will depend, are Reich's symbolic analysts. While most material needs can be satisfied by manufacturing processes that are largely automated, improvement in the quality of life will stem from the application of intellectual energy to innovation and the tailoring of products and services to rapidly changing technologies and needs. The speed of creation of knowledge accelerates, calling for continuous updating of products and services as well as the skills of those who provide them; hence the rise of consultancy, of professional services and of management in recent years; hence too the growth of small specialist companies catering to niche markets.

In this world, the kowledge and skills imparted through higher education will both play a growing part, and the ability to apply them to unfamiliar contexts becomes essential. The creation, analysis and dissemination of knowledge has always been the central function of higher education, and the institutions of higher education (universities, disciplinary and professional bodies) have played a central role in determining what kinds of knowledge will carry value and status. However, higher education has traditionally regarded some kinds of knowledge as superior, or perhaps more interesting, than others. In most, though not all, spheres it has valued the theoretical more highly than the practical, with status rising in proportion to the distance from application. The result has been a devaluing of the practical skills which higher education gives its learners (communication, writing, working in groups), and a failure to develop these fully. It has also resulted in a failure to develop to the full the potential links between the learners' life outside the walls and inside them.

My final aspect of change is in the nature of organizations. At all levels of society, at least in the English-speaking economies, the pressure is to reduce rather than enlarge. The past decade has seen a rapid growth in the numbers of small firms in Britain. Some 94 per cent of all British firms employ fewer than ten people (HMSO 1995), and half the non-public sector workforce works in firms smaller than 100 people (up from 40 per cent in 1979). This change has come from two directions: the growth of new kinds of small firm – freelance, consultancy, professionals and personal services – and the fragmentation of the large organizations. The giants of the past like ICI and GEC subdivide, contract out many specialized services and enter into new kinds of partnership with other agencies, in this country and abroad. It is ironic that during this period almost the only kind of organization which has grown in size is the university. Some of the largest institutions in Britain are now universities. Three of the five largest employers in the North-East are universities (Goddard *et al.* 1994), and almost no other organization involves the 15,000–20,000 people in a single city which is the typical civic university. But observed more closely, universities are themselves very fragmented organizations, whose size is only tenable because they comprise many, largely autonomous, sub-units – faculties, schools, departments, disciplines, course teams – bound together by a range of complex and delicate relationships.

The new organizations have shorter lives than the old ones. The technologies on which they depend have shorter life cycles; they depend less on long-term investment in plant and in human communities, and much more on the vagaries of the market and the talents of key people. The recent history of the advertising industry (one of Britain's more successful service industries) demonstrates how many very successful firms are built around the skills of a handful of people, on whose personal loyalty their survival depends. If the key people go, so does the business. Such organizations also require different skills of all their employees, and need faster and more practical responses to new demands, better political and collaborative skills, and a greater sensitivity to opportunity and risk.

Alongside this, the speed of technological change makes whole occupations and organizations obsolete, while the need to find ways of applying emerging technologies creates a constantly growing demand for new services and skills. Few, if any, people will continue to work in the same field with the same employer for a working life (whatever that may mean). Thus the notion of 'career' becomes more personal, and more complex. The art of career management will lie at least as much in the entrepreneurial skills of developing one's skills and knowledge and seeing opportunities to sell them in an ever changing market place, as in selecting a career path and following a planned promotion route. In the English-speaking economies at least, employers seem likely to be less supportive of individuals and make fewer long-term commitments.

For higher education these changes pose a series of challenges. Its social and economic roles are under threat from several directions at once. Others are bidding for its role in the creation and validation of knowledge, new qualities and capabilities are required of its graduates, the knowledge base on which it survives is changing more rapidly.

A changing higher education

Alongside these changes in the environment, higher education itself has been changing rapidly. The most conspicuous change of the late 1980s and early 1990s was in size: at the time of the Robbins Report most universities numbered their students in hundreds; the typical university now provides for 15,000 or more students. Driven by a government commitment to expanding participation, expressed in a funding methodology which rewarded expansion at the price of a declining unit of resource, many universities grew exponentially in the late 1980s. The need to respond to the huge pressures which this has put on resources and individuals was part of the rationale for the NIACE paper.

However, in the longer term, the shift in the profile of the student body may prove as important as the change in size. In 1988 mature students were, for the first time, a majority of entrants to higher education in England and Wales, and after 1990 their numbers continued to rise when recruitment of school leavers was capped for financial reasons (significantly, the policy of 'consolidation' was announced in a budget speech, not by the Secretary of State for Education). Alongside this ageing of the student body, we have also seen a disproportionate growth in postgraduate and post-experience provision: lifelong higher education has begun to be a reality.

The shift towards a market model of post-school education has been under way for many years, but accelerated in the 1980s, as institutions were encouraged to compete for student numbers, and to enhance their income through full cost programmes for employers and postgraduates. Universities have been encouraged to see each other as competitors, and the rise of mass higher education has led them to become more sensitive to the demands of their customers, including students and employers. However, as in other areas where market systems have been introduced into overwhelmingly publicly funded services, the elaborate structure of regulation required to control the market has itself generated confusing, and sometimes perverse, signals (as, arguably, with the relative status of 'teaching' and 'research').

This need to respond to market pressures, combined with growing resource pressures, has led to the development of new and more flexible models of provision. There has been some, albeit modest, growth of open learning, of tailored courses and work-based learning, and of new kinds of partnership with other education agencies and employers. There has been a rapid expansion of higher education in further education institutions as well as the workplace. There has been a surge of modularization in most universities, sometimes accompanied with the development of more flexible curricula, semesterization and credit transfer, although these have been uneven in both spread and quality.

A vision: the key traditions

It is easy to see these changes as a set of unrelated pressures, and for many within the system they have meant ever growing difficulties in trying to deliver the same service to larger numbers with fewer resources. The external pressures of new quality assurance processes and mechanisms for accountability have often seemed the straw to break the camel's back.

The NIACE paper sought, *post hoc*, to create a coherent picture from the apparent confusion of initiatives, and to outline a vision of what a new higher education might look like, drawing on the experience of these changes, and the likely social and economic needs of Britain in the next century. There were several reasons for NIACE to do this. The common strands of change focus strongly on the adult dimension of higher education: lifelong learning is beginning to take a hold, and has now been formally recognized by government in the UK and throughout the developed world (DfEE 1995); mature learners are the majority; a growing proportion of learners are studying alongside and in breaks in work; the economy is increasingly driven by knowledge and high-level skills. On top of this, workplaces are becoming more like places of learning, actively encouraged by initiatives like the government's Investors in People, while higher education is becoming more like the workplace, with increasing traffic in ideas and people between the two.

The first question which the NIACE group asked was what aspects of the traditions of British higher education must be preserved at all costs. It would be foolish to sacrifice a well deserved high reputation in favour of a mere transitory innovation. We identified two strands. The first comes from the old world. It is the British tutorial tradition, which places the face-to-face relationship between tutor and learner at the centre of the education process. A more diverse and mature student body, and an economy which will rest on the special talents of individuals, rather than mass produced bodies of knowledge, will need to develop individual talents and enthusiasms in the way for which the tutorial relationship is particularly well suited. The second area for recovery and preservation is the civic tradition: of a higher education responsive to its local communities, which comes from the foundation of the great civic universities, and was carried forward by the polytechnics. In this model higher education feeds both into and on its local and regional communities, gathering and developing ideas and helping those communities to use them. This rooting of higher education in the personal relationship of teacher and learner, and in a sense of responsibility to its region, seemed to us central to a vision of the future.

Of the two, the civic tradition is probably the more healthy, speaking more obviously to the agenda of the 1980s. The development of 'cities of learning' and proposals for new universities (Lincolnshire, the Lakes) based on explicit linkage between higher education and social and economic regeneration demonstrate that the civic tradition is alive and well in some places, but by no means all. On the other hand, despite its links to the development of individualized learning and flexible workers, the tutorial tradition is more evidently expensive in staff resource, and has fared less well. In some places it has been abandoned, while in other 'tutorial' groups have grown beyond a point where the original purpose can be easily achieved. There is growing evidence that students are finding it more difficult to engage with higher education, deprived of this personal dimension (Moore 1995). Ironically, many young people now progress from a strongly individualized and personal sixth form education to an individualized workplace, by way of a very large and impersonal higher education institution. If an essential part of higher education is the development and shaping of personal knowledge through direct debate between individuals, we must find ways of reviving it, if necessary at the cost of other priorities. The argument for doing so is strengthened by the evidence from international comparisons about the economic benefits of combining the individualist (tutorial) traditions of Western societies with the collectivist (civic) traditions of the East. It is those societies which have managed this combination that have most evidently thrived in the past decades (Hampden *et al.* 1992).

Six principles

From these foundations the NIACE paper identified six principles on which a new model of higher education might be built. First, if 'higher' means anything, it must be a kind of education, rather than a kind of institution. Not all that goes on in universities is 'higher', and not all that is 'higher' goes on in universities. Increasingly, higher-level learning happens outside the walls, and some commercial firms now publish more refereed academic research than the average university. There is, however, an active debate about whether 'higher' really has any meaning. Some argued for an integrated model, where higher and further education are merged into a single sector, while others took the view that, without some recognition of the special qualities of higher education, something valuable might be at risk, and that, at best, a new and damaging hierarchy of status would develop. If creating a new 'tertiary' sector by bringing together further and higher education institutions merely provided the means for a select handful of 'old' universities to reassert their status as a smaller elite than before, the result would be more divisive than the pre-1992 structure.

However, it is easier to argue for the unique qualities of higher education than to define them, and the nearest we came was that the distinguishing characteristic lies in the relationship between the creation of knowledge and its transmission as the core of the higher education experience. This can be seen most clearly in the notion of the 'ownership' of the knowledge base. Typically in further education and schools, it is assumed that the question of what is to be learned, and what is valuable, is made outside the institution (by government, employers, awarding bodies, lead bodies etc.); in higher education, on the other hand, it is made within the institution, the discipline or profession, and students can, from a relatively early stage in some disciplines, be actively involved in the processes of debate and creation.

The second principle is that higher education should be lifelong, not initial. The world in which the dominant role of higher education is the completion of the initial education of the children of the middle classes is gone. In future we must assume that more diverse people will enter, and that most of those who complete their initial experience of higher education will return, perhaps to an institution of higher education, to continue their learning careers, or at least to undertake learning at that level independently. It then becomes essential to consider what is best learned at the initial stage, when foundations are laid, and what might be pursued later. Such an approach has the potential to take some pressure off the first degree curriculum, increasingly overcrowded as universities strive to pack more and more knowledge into the first three years of what should be conceived as a lifelong process. The evolution of the bodies of knowledge will continue as a long-term project for the academic community and society at large, but the individual will be dipping in and out repeatedly, and much of the learning which builds on the core of the discipline will be delivered in small units to people returning repeatedly over a lifetime.

Third, a new higher education would be student-centred: built around the needs, ambitions and talents of individual learners. The economic need is for adaptable individuals with transferable skills and personal commitment of the kind which comes from fostering individual talent rather than mass delivery. It is here that the processes of negotiation, familiar to the adult education tradition, come to the fore. We also see a central role for the tutor, helping the individual to map a learning career through an increasingly diverse range of learning opportunities, and to produce a result which is intellectually coherent and personally relevant. It is a model which will call for more flexible and diverse forms of delivery, some of which may prove more economical, and, since they build on the intrinsic motivation of the individual, make better use of the learner's energies.

The new system will also be achievement-led. We still have an intensely hierarchical society, and much of the status structure of British higher education rests on the need to demonstrate one person's or institution's success through the failure of others. For many years, the quality of a course was measured not by the success of its graduates, but by the number of people who failed to get into it. It is a model challenged fundamentally by recent developments in both vocational education and schooling, where the attempt to define explicit criteria for success creates the heretical possibility of everyone succeeding. Higher education, meanwhile, continues to be dominated by exclusive models, as if telling learners what they have to learn is unethical, although the evidence is that when the objectives are clear individuals are more motivated and effective, even in those areas where definition is difficult and contested.

A new HE would also be economically proactive. Since many of its learners will be in employment, they will bring with them problems and issues from the outside world, while young students completing their initial education are increasingly involved in work placements and experience as part of their degrees. Such movement of people carries with it ideas and knowledge, often unrecognized in a world where 'technology transfer' is presumed to mean leading edge and revolutionary technologies. Yet many of the most important economic benefits of higher education come from this transfer of ideas at the level of the individual learner and worker, tailoring established ideas and technologies to new circumstances. The information technology skills of the averagely computer literate undergraduate, taken with them through placements and part-time work, can be of as much value to many small firms as the leading edge technologies being developed through research.

A more open and democratic higher education would be more explicit about its purposes, outcomes and processes. It would seek to describe these in terms comprehensible to potential students, employers and the general public, enabling individuals to make wise choices about increasingly complex and personal learning careers, and enabling employers and government to understand the relevance of particular qualifications to particular needs. This is not an easy process, since the outcomes of higher education are complex and difficult to describe, but the task of making them explicit is being recognized by a growing number of universities, who see it as worth the effort in order to strengthen the commitment, and improve the learning, of individual learners, confident about the route they have chosen, and clear about how success will be demonstrated.

Finally, an adult higher education will be diverse, in its institutions, programmes and learners. Higher education will seek to meet many needs – of individuals, employers, the state – and different players will be involved at different times and places. Institutions should not, therefore, be crammed into pursuing a single model. However, it is important that this diversity should not be merely a device to ensure the survival of traditional and damaging institutional hierarchies. The mechanisms for describing the performance and identity of institutions should thus be multidimensional, and seek to express the particular purposes and strengths of each institution, rather than establishing their position on a single ladder.

Frameworks

The NIACE paper developed these principles into a structural model. It proposed that institutions should be thought of in terms of three broad functional areas, underpinned by two infrastructural elements.

The first functional area was a framework for 'learner support', embracing all the mechanisms which enable the individual to engage with the learning, including tutoring, educational and careers guidance. Here the central issues are to do with definitions and roles: whose job is it to help individuals to find their place in the institution, to map their learning routes and plan their future beyond the walls? How do the various professional groups relate to each other? How can the tutorial function, under such pressure from increased numbers, be preserved?

The second area was curriculum. Here there are key issues about the balance between core or generic qualities and specialist knowledge. It has been widely argued that the qualities which individuals will require to thrive in the new economy are as much generic skills like analysis and communication, albeit at a high level, as specialist knowledge (CBI 1992; Harvey *et al.* 1994). However, the transmission of specialist knowledge and skills is a key function of the university, which must not be lost in a rush to guarantee long neglected core skills. It is also unclear at what point in a lifelong learning career people can best acquire different kinds of knowledge. Many institutions already offer a curriculum which concentrates on generic qualities in the early stages, leading to greater specialization later. The current reform of medical education, with a strong shift towards problem, rather than knowledge, centred learning in the early stages is a case in point. Such approaches call, however, for new strategies for planning and ensuring coherence in the curriculum, as do modular and other flexible curricula: balance and timing become more important issues.

The third area is 'credit', embracing the processes of measuring achievement and awarding qualifications, increasingly for smaller units of achievement – for modules, units or elements. The key issues here are coherence: how do we ensure that individuals do not unwittingly construct learning programmes which make no sense to them or to the world outside, without imposing a rigidity of regulation which would stifle growth and creativity within the system? An important part of this is the development of more relevant and economical approaches to assessment, perhaps the thing which higher education generally does least imaginatively (Atkins 1993). Modularization and greater emphasis on core and transferable skills is leading in many institutions to problems of over-assessment, a trend which may be exacerbated as elements of National Vocational Qualifications (which require assessment of all elements, rather than the sampling which is normal in higher education) begin to be incorporated into degrees.

Traditionally, these three functions have been undertaken by the same staff. Academics are expected to be good at helping individuals to find their way through the learning experience, at transmitting knowledge and developing skills, and at assessing the outcomes. It is not surprising that some elements are less well done than one would like, and not all academics are comfortable with the role. Just as the introduction of NVQs at lower levels has led to the separation of assessment from teaching, so the functions might be disaggregated in higher education – as the Robertson Report suggested, we might see the growth of a specialist profession of guidance workers, or of specialist assessors (Robertson 1994a).

These three elements relate directly to the learning of students. But they rest on two key infrastructures. The first is quality assurance, all those processes by which the quality of what takes place is guaranteed. Whatever the mechanism adopted, the principle must be that all quality assurance is the property not only of the institutions themselves, but of the community which they serve, including learners, employers and the wider community. In the long term the failure of current quality assurance systems to pay adequate attention to these audiences may prove a serious mistake in terms of political support and accountability. Accountability should not be simply a matter of external measuring, or of academic introspection. Rather, we should be seeking an ongoing dialogue between providers and users, a constant refining of objectives, and clarifying of how their delivery is to be properly measured. In this way higher education would bring its stakeholders into the community of higher education as partners, rather than holding them at arm's length, as dangerous outsiders (who happen to hold the purse strings).

The second element of infrastructure is funding. Present mechanisms for funding are inadequate and inequitable. They have delivered the planned expansion of participation, but at a heavy cost to the unit of resource, which has eroded key elements of the higher education experience. They discriminate in favour of full-time students (overwhelmingly young people) at the expense of part-timers (overwhelmingly adult), they continue to subsidize the living costs of young people from general taxation. The present loan scheme, as work at the London School of Economics has pointed out, fails the test of sound finance, or efficiency or equity, discouraging participation and increasing student poverty (Barr and Falkingham n.d.). The artificial division of funding between teaching and research discourages creative interaction between the two, and distracts some staff from teaching and broader scholarship. NIACE argued that we should seek to fund through smaller and more flexible units, perhaps through some form of voucher scheme, and that the maintenance award should be abolished, to be replaced by a generally available, properly structured loan scheme, accessible to all learners, and repayable through the National Insurance or tax system. The evidence is that most informed politicians understand the need for such radical reform, but fear alienating powerful constituencies by admitting it. Sadly, the 1995 Budget suggests that government is unwilling, or unable, to present the electorate with such a strategy.

The dilemma

The publication of the NIACE paper was followed by extensive written consultation, and a series of meetings and conferences. There was strong endorsement for the principle of articulating a coherent vision, and most respondents also endorsed the principles. However, respondents pointed to a number of outstanding issues in need of attention, of which the most critical were perhaps funding and quality. As many pointed out, unless we can solve the funding dilemma the principles will have no meaning.

The policy dilemma is very clear. We want more, and more diverse, people to have access, we want to maintain the quality of what is provided, and we want to do this with shrinking public funds. The equation does not add up, and the broad thrust of many of the responses to the NIACE paper was that all three elements are being eroded quietly while we fail to face some hard choices. It is therefore worth exploring these three elements and asking what is essential, and what can be either abandoned or reframed to meet a new context.

To abandon the principle of expanding access would be both foolish and wrong. The knowledge-based economy will need more graduate-level skills, and experience of expansion does not suggest that we have exhausted the pool of people who could benefit from higher education (though we have reached the different point at which we do not need more graduates to fill the traditional style of elite graduate jobs). Nor is the argument for 'graduate oversupply' defensible. It may be the case that we are producing more graduates than a depressed and under performing economy can take up, but, as Keep and Mayhew (1995) have argued, one of Britain's historical weaknesses has always been its inclination to reduce quality and aim for the bottom end of markets in order to match production to the low skills and expectations of its workers. In a global labour market, where Britain can never hope to compete on price alone, it is a strategy doomed to failure, and in a world where access to work and wealth is likely to depend increasingly on high-level knowledge and skills it would be morally indefensible to deny initial access to higher education (whatever that means) to those capable of benefiting from it.

However, public funding of higher education is not likely to expand: no political party is proposing it, and alternative private sources must clearly be explored, including a more rational use of loans to enable individuals to spread the costs across a lifetime, rather than concentrating them in the early years of a career, when they are most difficult to meet.

Quality is a slippery but vital element of the equation. Historically, British higher education has a high and deserved reputation, but we have real difficulty in defining what we mean by quality, and how we might measure it in the new, more diverse system. The responses to *An Adult Higher Education* are not the only body of evidence suggesting scepticism about whether our present quality assurance processes are measuring the most critical aspects of the quality of higher education, and whether they are involving all the relevant interests effectively. Many people commented that the quality of the student's experience has declined, although the quality of the individual components may not have evidently suffered – a good lecture remains a good lecture, but if it replaces a good tutorial the quality of the learner's experience will have changed, and probably been diminished. The Higher Education Quality Council's current work on 'standards' is seeking to address part of this question, but it is difficult to see how this can produce consensus about the standard of such an amorphous notion as the honours degree, across all institutions and subjects. More likely, perhaps, is the development of some kind of common core of skills across degree programmes, but this too is contentious: we do not yet understand how transferable skills like 'problem-solving' or 'communication' really are, when applied across such diverse fields as microbiology, history and work in a small manufacturing or consulting firm.

Initial higher education is a system under great and increasing pressure. The traditional first degree has become unmanageable because we have failed to recognize the implications of lifelong learning. The curriculum is overcrowded because we have been seeking to provide everything which an individual needs before the age of 21, despite the fact that much of the knowledge will be obsolete in a few years (if not months). It is also anachronistic. The benchmark is a degree model designed to produce embryo academics rather than lifelong learners or effective workers, despite: the fact that the system now caters for over 40 per cent of the population (assuming a 30 per cent youth participation rate and an equal number of mature participants); the fact that a high proportion of graduates do not go into employment directly related to their first degree discipline (even in strongly 'vocational' fields it often does not reach 50 per cent, as is indicated in work carried out by the DfEE funded Pharmacology Discipline network); and the fact that mature graduates are experiencing age discrimination in the labour market. Furthermore, we have grafted on to this model, with varying degrees of commitment and success, attempts at increasing flexibility and accessibility, many of which put old structures, and staff, under great stress.

Towards a new model?

In the light of the responses to the NIACE consultation my view of the answer is twofold. We must not, for economic or moral reasons, abandon the access goals. But the price will have to be to accept a greater individual contribution to the costs (bearing in mind that 40 per cent of higher education students now pay their own fees – for part-time and postgraduate courses). We must abolish the anachronistic maintenance award system, which discriminates against the mature and the part-time, and increasingly against those from lower socio-economic groups. The question is then how the balance of public and private funding is distributed.

My answer to the question is that to attempt to spread the current funding more thinly across the same curriculum offer is a recipe for declining quality and demoralized staff and students. Rather, I suggest, we should review the structure of higher education qualifications, and recognize that, in practice, higher education involves two distinct, if overlapping, phases of activity. The first is a foundation of study at higher level, reflecting at its best the generic skills of 'graduateness' as well as a solid foundation for lifelong learning. Here there is a clear public interest in securing the maximum participation, and consequently a strong case for public funding. The second is more specialized, a training for specific work in the high-skill 'knowledge-based' industries (including academic work). For some people this study follows immediately on from the foundation stage, for some it is undertaken part-time or in short bursts later in life in response to changing personal circumstances, changes in work and social roles. Here the balance of benefit shifts substantially towards the individual and the employer, and the case for a substantial private contribution is much stronger.

We have, of course, such a distinction now. The first degree aims to meet the first need, while a rather incoherent bundle or provision known as 'postgraduate', 'post-experience', 'continuing' and 'professional updating' forms the second. But I would argue that the boundary between the two stages is not adequately defined; nor is it located at the right point (the end of the honours degree). It is not clear that we need three years full-time (or its 'equivalent' part-time) to complete the first phase adequately, and if this were to be shorter, it would be easier to fund it effectively and guarantee its quality, not as the answer to a lifetime's higher education needs, but the first stage of a lifetime learning career. A shorter initial qualification might prove both cheaper and better.

What would such a qualification look like? First, it should guarantee the development, at a high level, of the generic and core skills which make people employable in a knowledge-based economy. Second, it would provide an induction into serious higher-level learning in a discipline. While the degree would be a more generic qualification, it would, like first degrees now, be based in a discipline (or group of disciplines). The 'graduate' of a foundation programme in chemistry would know what it is like to think like a chemist, what kinds of proof a chemist's arguments require and how to analyse and criticize work in the field. It should also include an understanding of how to place chemistry in a broader social, economic and political setting, in order to enable those who become chemists to do so in a socially responsible and ethical context, and those who do not to understand some of the arguments and debates on which they may, as educated citizens of a democracy, be called to make judgements.

Such a qualification would not be an easy option, but it need not take three years of full-time study. The radical solution is to create a new foundation higher education qualification, whose quality is more consistently and rigorously maintained across all higher education, and which might be equivalent in volume to perhaps two years of the present first degree (not the present three years crammed into two, which has been explored through the AIRs project) (HEFCE 1996). This would then be supplemented by a larger and more diverse range of second level qualifications and programmes, which might be taken 'end on' or pursued later in life as the needs arose. The addition of post-foundation qualifications would increase the flexibility of the system, make it easier to cope with the pressures for international comparability (where the credibility of the English model, previously based on high selection and the intensive residential three-year model, looks increasingly tenuous) and provide a better guarantee of the core skills and capabilities which employers repeatedly say they want, and fail to get, in graduates. By reducing the 'size' of such qualifications it would be possible to guarantee access to larger numbers and to provide a guarantee of real quality.

Such a move follows trends already established in many universities (for example, the three-phase curriculum model adopted by Sheffield Hallam University), but the replacement of the three-year honours degree will be viewed with great suspicion by many (some of the arguments are explored in Robertson 1994b). Those who advocate it have to be sure that the savings made by a fundamental reshaping can be diverted into improving access and quality, and not clawed back by the Treasury. But those who oppose it have to be very sure that we are not on a slippery slope where access, quality and funding are all deteriorating in order to preserve a qualifications structure which no longer meets the needs of society, the economy or lifelong learners.

References

Atkins, M. (1993) *Assessment Issues in Higher Education*. Sheffield, Department of Employment.

Barr, N. and Falkingham, J. (n.d.) *Paying for Learning*. London, LSE Welfare State Programme.

CBI (1992) *Towards a Skills Revolution*. London, CBI.

Department for Education and Employment (1995) *Lifetime Learning: a Consultation Document*. Sheffield, DfEE.

Goddard, J. *et al.* (1994) *Universities and Their Communities*. London, CVCP.

Hampden-Turner, C. and Trompenaars, F. (1993) *The Seven Cultures of Capitalism*. New York, Doubleday.

Harvey, L. *et al.* (1994) *Someone Who Can Make an Impression*. Birmingham, QHE Project, University of Central England.

HMSO (1995) *Small Firms in Britain*. London, HMSO.

Keep, E. and Mayhew, K. (1995) Training policy for competitiveness – time for a fresh perspective, in H. Metcalf (ed.) *Future Skill Demand and Supply*. London, PSI.

Moore, R. (1995) *Retention Rates Project Final Report*. Sheffield, Sheffield Hallam University.

NIACE (1990) *Adults in Higher Education*. Leicester, NIACE.

NIACE (1991) *An Adult Higher Education*. Leicester, NIACE.

Robertson, D. (1994a) *Choosing to Change*. London, HEQC.

Robertson, D. (1994b) Proposals for an associate degree – the search for the missing link in British higher education, *Higher Education Quarterly*, 48(4): 294–322.

Sims, L. and Woodrow, M. (1996) *Fast and Flexible: the AIRs Experience; the Evaluation of the Accelerated and Intensive Routes to Higher Education*. Bristol, HEFCE.

7

Repositioning Higher Education

Bill Williamson and Frank Coffield

Support your universities.
> (Association of University Teachers banner, 25 June 1996)

Universties are for posh fucking bastards.
> (Graffito in Durham)

Introduction

As the millennium approaches, higher education in Britain is in turmoil. There are too many students for the resources available. Institutions face further, systematic erosion of their resources, with the strong likelihood of both staff losses through early retirement and redundancy coupled with staff shortages as the decade comes to a close. Students face the prospect of paying more for their higher education whichever government is in power, and no one can have confidence that the research capacity of universities will be maintained at the level required to keep Britain in the race to remain a modern, knowledge-based industrial society.

The Dearing Committee of Inquiry into higher education has not come too soon. Whether Dearing can succeed is entirely another matter, but his report may resolve a number of issues. His conclusions on lifelong learning, part-time degrees, student financial support and quality control can well be imagined, and if they are formulated clearly and backed up with appropriate resources, they will help enormously in strengthening progressive higher education and the long-term competitiveness of the British economy.

Three problems are likely to remain unaddressed. They concern the planning process itself, the nature of democratic citizenship and, finally, the management values and institutional flexibility of university institutions themselves. In this concluding chapter we hope to shift the terms of the debate about policy-making in higher education to escape the limitations of the current discourses which dominate them.

The market and the plan

In the United Kingdom there is an unresolvable contradiction between a market model of educational planning and one based on the plan. Conservative ministers of education have had few inhibitions in centralizing educational decision-making while simultaneously expressing their unashamed ideological commitment to the market and the local autonomy of institutions. Universities have lost much of their previous autonomy from government as they have been forced to compete for students and resources.

The strategy has resulted in a low-cost increase in student numbers and seriously underresourced institutions. Without doubt, should the same policies remain or intensify, the system of higher education in the United Kingdom will become a very divided one, with a few, large, research-based, prestigious institutions and a larger number of teaching-only colleges struggling to secure students and to find ways to fulfil their roles in education, training and local economic regeneration.

The resource base of the system is scheduled to erode despite the best efforts of colleges to raise more money from non-government sources. Universities have appointed public relations officers, hunted benefactors, staffed fund-raising development units and squeezed their alumni to the limits of their generosity. These efforts have had some success: the proportion of their income derived from non-government sources – with great variation among institutions – has increased year by year for the past decade. It is still not enough.

The real problem of finding resources adequate to the needs of a successful system of higher education remains untouched by these necessary but none the less short-term, palliative measures. It is to secure a flow of both public and private resources to institutions on the basis of the services they provide to a range of different communities of interest in society as a whole. At present, they are too often seen as serving the interests of only a small, privileged stratum of society.

Will the Dearing Report solve this problem? Will the process of higher education planning be robust enough to deal with it even if Dearing urges it to do so in positive and compelling ways? We suspect not, for Dearing, like Robbins over thirty years before, is working within a particular discourse and in a political framework – the British state itself – which is archaic and which responds best to the needs of the privileged and powerful in a society that continues to fail in the international league of industrial growth and competitition. It is telling that the terms of reference enjoin the National Committee of Inquiry to take account of 'the constraints of the Government's other spending priorities and affordability' (*DfEE News*, 10 May 1996).

Stability and change in the old model of higher education

The discourse is one which limits what can be achieved in education by myopic short-term calculations of its cost and which institutionalizes the assumption that higher education is essentially the preserve of the clever stratum of the younger generation. Dearing is asked explicitly to consider the needs of mature students and lifelong learning, but he will do so against a climate in which such developments will be read as additional demands on universities and not something which they should be engaged in as part of their central mission.

Progress in the past decade about widened access to higher education has had to be achieved through struggle against these assumptions. Even when they have been actively promoted by the University Grants Committee (as in its 1984 report) or the Department for Education and Science, the rationale for change has always been couched in terms of increasing the supply of students to a system which was expected to retain its form despite growth in numbers.

Arguments in favour of lifelong learning and the accessible university have been met by the objection that such developments must be funded by individuals themselves, and by the business community, even against the evidence that UK business has an appalling record of training and of invest-ment in education and training. Without a longer-term strategy for educa-tion and training which rests on a legislative agreement between government, employers, individuals and universities to commit them to a strong and forward-looking partnership, to boost this country's brainpower, reports like the one expected from Sir Ron Dearing will result in little real change. David Robertson (this volume) has articulated this demand as one requir-ing a renegotiated contract between higher education and society.

The capacity of the British state to constrain innovation and reform within a tight and short-term financial framework is only part of the problem. There is also the wider question of an atrophied political imagination to be considered. In *The Culture of Contentment*, as Galbraith (1992) has described it, politicians are driven to deliver low taxes to the contented majority in the mass electorate. This is the one issue that dominates all political debate in the United Kingdom.

As politics itself becomes a spectacle played out on the media, political success comes to depend more and more on the clever sound-bite or the short-term benefit of voting for one party rather than another. As the histor-ical opposition of organized labour to the forces of capital is diluted, or is accommodated into the political system itself, radical debate about the future shape of society is stifled or marginalized.

Universities are implicated in this. They are valued insofar as they pro-mote the private welfare or financial future of individuals or achieve the short-term economic goals of the state. Their wider and longer-term public role is not clearly enough perceived or understood. Even less appreciated is the role they could play in defence of democratic values and in nurturing the critical intelligence on which a modern democracy rests. The dominant discourse – discussed in the first chapter of this volume – in higher education planning is concerned with resources, cost-effectiveness in public expenditure, accountability, monitored standards, performance targets and human capital theory. Its legitimating rhetoric is that of the market place and its values are those of competitive individual achievement. The process of educational decision-making and planning is itself a reflection both of this discourse and the contradictions in it.

Institutions are expected to improve their resources in competition with others. The use of a bidding process to allocate resources to institutions is a device to impose uniformity of resource on a system while claiming to celebrate the diversity of different missions. Resources follow students, but student choice is something of a myth when central government, through the Higher Education Funding Councils, restricts places at institutions through the tight control of maximum aggregate student numbers (MASN).

This is a top-down model of educational planning dependent on expert advice which can be relied upon to be pragmatic and responsible. It is a system which pays lip service to the institutional autonomy of universities and forces upon them at a local level the task of managing the contradictions of the national policies themselves. If they fail in the task, then the blame rests clearly on their own shoulders. The result is that universities in Britain cannot plan their own development effectively despite being required to do so. They are given impossibly tight student numbers targets. Their capital and equipment expenditure is held under strict control or reduced. The limits of their freedom, with the exception of the ancient universities, are tightly set. It is unlikely that Dearing will be able to break free of this mould or dare to think outside it, for his recommendations have to be couched in terms of what is politically acceptable and in a conventional sense practicable and 'affordable'.

The task facing people in higher education is to think beyond the constraints of conventional wisdom. If universities are to respond to the challenges and uncertainties of the new century, they must find fresh ways to do so. The old frameworks for planning and managing them are no longer fit for repositioning them for the new century.

R. H. Tawney (1981) noted in his 1917 essay, 'A national college of all souls' – a plea for a national system of education as the most appropriate memorial for those who died on the Somme during the First World War – that only those institutions which touch the imagination are loved. He compared British education at the time to a post box. It was functional but uninspiring. Those who died in the First World War did so in defence of the values of democratic civilization. The only fitting way to acknowledge their sacrifice was through the development of social institutions, particularly in education, which reflected the ideals they died for. Fifty years on from another World War and, as the century draws to its close, Tawney's argument still has force. Against strong utilitarian views of the purposes of higher education it is vital to assert the importance of different values and to conceive of forms of higher education which do excite the imagination and in which it is acknowledged that millions of people have contributed to their survival and success, not just the privileged few who benefit directly from them.

The challenge to do so is not just an economic one. At the centre of it, as the twentieth century itself showed, is the need to develop strong defences against the forces and values which erode democracy. The task is for higher education to play its part in building the kind of society which achieves a high quality of life for *all* its members in ways which are consistent with the care of a sustainable natural environment and a stable order of international relationships.

We have to imagine a society whose higher education institutions contribute to these wider goals within the public realm and whose own systems of management reflect the values of a civilized and democratic society. Current political discourse about higher education has barely touched on these questions. The result is that universities in the United Kingdom face the future with considerable uncertainty and precarious public support.

To a significant extent, universities have themselves to blame for being in this position. As we argued earlier in this volume, they have been too ready to defend or simply live with an older model of what higher education should be. This is not a new argument. Maurice and David Kogan (1983) castigated senior university staff for simply caving in against the cuts imposed by the Thatcher government in 1981 because many were ambivalent about defending a system which was trying to expand and broaden the social basis of its intake.

There has been a great deal of clever talk about how institutions can modernize and change. Much has been written about the postmodern university reacting flexibly to the needs of a fragmented society in an era which has lost its faith in the great narrative themes of progress and science (Scott 1995). There is an industry growing up around information technology and the new modes of learning it could sustain. Each week the educational journals are filled with futuristic scenarios of the disembedded university serving students at a distance through the Internet.

Much, indeed, has been achieved in this field. Students now leave college computer literate. Electronic databases have revolutionized the search for information and communication among scholars and researchers. Open distance learning packages meet an increasing range of student needs for learning. The Open University is one of the most successful public institutions of modern Britain.

The technology of communication, however, is about the means through which learning can be facilitated. The values which inform learning and education still have to be articulated and defended. This can only be done in full awareness of what is happening to modern society and against a critical understanding of the forces which threaten its democratic values.

It is in this area of debate that the discussion of the future of higher education has been at its weakest.

Universities need to reposition themselves in modern society if they are to contribute to these debates and ensure their own survival as institutions. The new century will see an intensification of the developments which extend the global economy, tighten the bonds between knowledge and power and weaken further the fiscal base of modern states. The distinctive research role of universities could well erode as new forms of knowledge generation and dissemination develop in the vast, global markets of the knowledge-based economy (Gibbons *et al.* 1994). The implications of these changes for the role, function and form of higher education institutions will be profound. Some will certainly not survive; others will be transformed. Internationally prestigious institutions, like Oxford and Cambridge, Harvard or the Grandes Ecoles in France, are likely to remain at the pinnacle of their national systems and retain much of their present institutional identity.

Whether higher education will play a strong role in developing an economically successful and democratic society remains, however, an open question. Which interests will dominate as the new century unfolds is something to be actively debated now.

Universities have been responsive to changes in their global environment. They have been active in international programmes of student exchange and research. In Britain and in Europe there is a growing framework of cooperation among academic institutions. Yet universities are still not safe. They remain under threat of further resource cuts and constant pressure to dance to the tunes of governments. In divided societies like this, where the political imperative is for people to pay less tax, governments are unlikely to support calls for more resources for higher education. Indeed, it can be strongly argued that the social rates of return to investment in education would be much greater if more was spent on nursery education or primary schools or on initiatives to improve the job chances of 16–19-year-olds (see Keep and Mayhew 1995).

If the institution of the university does not excite the imagination of its potential students or is not central to how people construct their lifelong careers, it will remain at the mercy of the politician and the short-term economic plan. The immediate task for those who work in universities, and particularly for those with a responsibility to manage them, is to be clear on what the future challenges will be and to debate them now. A new kind of dialogue is required which broadens out the discussion of these matters from the narrow utilitarian discourse which has dominated them to date.

Rising to the challenge

If universities did not already exist, they would have to be invented. What is less certain is that modern societies would choose to develop the kinds of institutions which they presently have. As the twentieth century draws to a close, the weaknesses of the current models of higher education, as the essays in this volume have shown, are clear. The 'donnish dominion' (Halsey 1992) has declined and in the postmodern redrawing of the map of knowledge, universities are no longer at the centre of the 'new production of knowledge' (Gibbons *et al.* 1994).

Were they to lose their chartered monopoly to validate learning through accreditation, their present role as guardians of intellectual standards could be easily usurped. Indeed, with the growth of professional accreditation and institutions like the National Council for Vocational Qualifications in Britain, it is already happening.

Starved of resources, their capacity to innovate, which has never been to the fore, could be squeezed out of them. As they are players in an academic market place which is increasingly global in its competitiveness, differences in the status and resources of universities could amplify well beyond those which currently exist. Some institutions could close; many more face amalgamation into larger units. Courses and study programmes structured to be delivered in particular places could easily be overtaken by those provided through the means of information technology on an open distance learning basis and provided by competitors elsewhere, some of them overseas.

Forced into a market place in which the services they provide have to be tailored to the needs of powerful stakeholders in government or industry, universities could well lose their ability to question critically the society in which they function. Who would then fill that small but essential critical space on which the fragile values of democracy depend? Which voices then would speak loudest in the already shrunken public realm of modern societies?

The challenges to higher education, then, are clear. One is to secure through public support those resources which will enable institutions to change in ways which provide for a sustainable commitment to education, to research and critical scholarship. Another is to find ways to play a strong role in helping people – not only full-time students, but people everywhere – to learn their way out of the problems they face in building a successful, just and democratic modern society.

The old models will no longer do. They met the needs of too few stakeholders and lack the widespread public support a system of higher education depends upon. Public funding, though essential, is not enough. Universities need to develop the capacity to become good at changing themselves and responding imaginatively and with foresight to the changes in society taking place around them.

Towards a new model

It is not possible to predict how higher education will change in the new century; the future of modern societies themselves is too uncertain. What is clear, however, is that there are no iron laws of history at work defining that future. Historicism – the belief that there are inexorable laws of history – was one of the great myths of the nineteenth and twentieth centuries. In the postmodernist re-evaluation of knowledge claims, our understanding of society and its institutions has to be reflexive.

This means acknowledging that social institutions are socially constructed and that the legitimacy of social institutions is something that has to be debated, fought for and secured. The ways of thinking which are woven into the social arrangements of a society are justified through a particular use of language and symbols. As Beare and Slaughter (1993) have argued, the ways in which people perceive their society are bound up with their experience and the roles they play within it.

What people think, therefore, is inextricably part of the resources of language, concepts and ideas available to them. This is not just true of ordinary members of society; it applies with equal force to the language of public policy and to the ways in which particular ideas about institutions, in this case universities, set limits on how people who work within them and manage them can conceive of them in the future. The old models of learning, scholarship and academic management still exercise a powerful influence on how universities function and limit their capacity to innovate and overcome the threats they face.

Knowing this, it is possible – indeed, it is incumbent on academic staff – to reconceive the dominant institutional models, to imagine alternative ways of organizing institutions of higher education. Beare and Slaughter (1993) go further; they suggest that to understand the present-day arrangements which prevail in education, it is necessary to imagine the different possibilities for change which the future might offer. In this way it is possible to escape from ways of thinking encoded in older models of the university and to identify more clearly what must change within them if a better future can be secured.

Two implications follow from this. The first is that we have to imagine at least some elements of how we would wish the future to be. In other words, we need to articulate different visions of higher education. Second, we have to negotiate the realization of these visions with those groups in society who have both the prime responsibility and the effective power to achieve them.

Key groups in this process include government, employers and the professions, the general public, higher education institutions themselves, management, unions and students. The system of higher education can be seen from this perspective as a negotiated order in which the interests of different groups in society for education, training and research struggle for power and acceptance.

This way of thinking brings questions of policy back into the realms of politics, removing them from the narrower domain of technical rationality. The key question is not how resources for higher education might be more effectively managed. The technical language of targets, mission statements and efficiency gains is, as we have shown in the first chapter, the language of industrial management. The discourse of managerial rationality of which it is a part has to be seen for what it is: an element of a dominant ideology which seeks to design a world fit for the global corporation. The ideological alchemy of it is to persuade us all that such a world would be fit for everyone to live in and that the kind of society we have now is rational, desirable and capable of reform from within if economic growth can be secured.

The key questions to be answered concern the kind of world we live in, the changes taking place in the structures of modern societies and the role to be played by higher education in responding to these changes. Reflecting on the 1995 UACE conference at Swansea, the theme of which was the university and the community, Jane Elliot and her colleagues (1996: xiii) have aptly noted the problem: 'universities will need to transform themselves from elitist institutions to ones significantly contributing to the creation of a more just and equitable society. Whether all can or wish to do so, is the great unanswered question.' Will they be in the mainstream or at the margins of social change? Will they play their part in the broad public debates about the future of modern society or will they remain tied to their older disciplinary and pedagogic concerns? Taking into account both the legacy of the past and realistic assessments of the risks faced by higher education in the future, the essential elements in our view, to reposition universities in the mainstream of public life, are as follows.

First and foremost, the institutions of higher education should be structured to nurture, examine critically and promulgate the values of a democratic society. Their fundamental normative commitment, without which their research and teaching functions become incoherent, is to the values of truthfulness, objectivity, freedom of thought and expression, personal integrity, honesty and democratic ways of working.

There is no comfort to be gained from the naive assumption that this is, in fact, what Western societies have achieved. The end of history may be celebrated, as Fukuyama (1993) has claimed, but what animates the festivities is a myth. The contrast was always between Western achievement and the totalitarian stagnation of the former Soviet bloc societies. As Vaclav Havel (1987) has pointed out, however, what Westerners saw in the wreckage of Eastern Europe – the pollution, the rape of nature, the distortion of science and scholarship to the needs of the state – was only an intensification of trends and potentialities inherent in Western society. The totalitarian system, he claimed, was ultimately 'a convex mirror of all modern civilization and a harsh, perhaps final call for a global recasting of that civilization's self understanding' (Havel 1987: 145). If not higher education, which institutions could possibly undertake such a task?

Second, the new responsibility of institutions of higher education is to facilitate the lifelong education of *all* citizens in the service of democracy rather than the initial education of an elite band of 18–21-year-olds (Duke in this volume). Through this they will contribute to the development of the social, cultural, intellectual and economic life of modern society. With a wider public purpose to what they do, they are more likely to enjoy wider public support.

Third, higher education institutions must remain accountable bodies in the public realm, serving legitimate and agreed public goals. This goal is not met by the bureaucratic procedures of quality control and of research selectivity currently in place in Britain. Both systems have been set up to evaluate the work of universities and secure improvements in its quality. The unintended consequences of these arrangements include, paradoxically, the reinforcement of the older academic model of higher education with its attendant elitism, subject-based research (which takes priority over teaching since academic careers depend on it) and burgeoning bureaucracy of an expensive, time-consuming kind. Middlehurst shows in this volume (Chapter 3) that it need not be like this. Quality control arrangements can be much more carefully designed to facilitate the growth of new kinds of courses and to enhance the learning experience of a much wider range of students.

Fourth, with the development and dissemination of knowledge as their central task, higher education institutions will, in the global economy of ideas, increasingly require a strong international outlook. Their capacity to serve the regions in which they are located will depend to a significant degree on their international status. They have to be simultaneously local and global in their intellectual reach.

The objective must be to fashion cooperative links among higher education institutions in particular regions and between them and the much more local further education colleges and secondary schools. They each contribute to the personal an professional development of people in the regions they serve. The irony and tragedy of existing funding arrangements for higher education in Britain is that institutions are pitted in pointless competition with one another to achieve a narrow range of goals, tied to student number targets and a narrow conception of subject-based research output. The roles they might play in serving their local communities and diverse constituencies within them are barely encouraged within the existing regimes of funding and control.

Despite this, there are many good examples of higher education institutions seeking innovative partnerships with local authorities and employers and local community interest groups. None the less, as Mohan (1996) has pointed out, these initiatives are neither well supported by the funding framework nor anything like as imaginative and effective as they could be. Both teaching and research models could be much more explicitly informed by a credo of education for democratic citizenship, for problem-solving and reflection and for much more direct involvement in a participatory way with the research and development needs of local communities.

Fifth, in a world of shifting intellectual boundaries and disciplinary fragmentation, institutions of higher education must promote forms of learning which are themselves inter-disciplinary and which enable students to be aware critically of the basis of all claims to knowledge and truth. Teaching must become dialogical rather than didactic and all learning should be closely geared to practice. Barnett, in this volume (Chapter 2), has set out what such learning could consist of and shown the ways in which it breaks out of the moulds of disciplinary logics and requires new kinds of relationships between the academy and society. A central thrust of all higher learning should be to equip students with a knowledge of how to learn. Such knowledge will help them meet the challenges of lifelong learning.

Sixth, higher education is not for everyone and cannot be compulsory. But it must be accessible (as Duke has argued, in Chapter 4) on a lifelong basis to all those who can benefit from it. School education was never sufficient to equip people to face the multiple challenges of their changing adult lives. In the global information economy its limitations are all too obvious. In a successful and just modern society adults require regular opportunities to develop their learning as a precondition of both continued employment and effective citizenship.

A new social contract is needed between employers and employees, based on employability rather than employment. The capacity of people to remain employable must be sustained through the continuous improvement of their skills and understanding, and higher education must play an active part in this.

Seventh, accessible institutions of higher education can no longer be constrained by the geography of their position or the time frames of an ecclesiastical calendar. New information technology, open distance learning and flexible curriculum models with credit accumulation and transfer will need to be combined to extend learning opportunities in ways students can take them up (Robertson, Chapter 5 in this volume). Courses to fit the new patterns of working life of both full-time and part-time workers are needed and this will require new patterns of work for academic staff.

New technology is part of the solution to problems like these, offering the prospect of flexible patterns of learning. Governments will embrace new learning technology with enthusiasm. So, too, will the multimedia, global information technology corporations which produce and sell it. Access to such technology is, however, unequal. Its planned use in higher education requires, therefore, strict criteria to ensure that its use does not generate new patterns of social exclusion.

Care will be needed to ensure that, within the creative use of the communication possibilities to be opened up, there is no dilution of that iconoclastic, critical commitment to truthfulness and objectivity which is at the heart of any credible idea of the university and the forms of dialogue it should sustain.

Eighth, higher education institutions should reflect in the structures of their own management the moral purposes for which they exist. The flexibility and democracy they require in their structures of management presuppose a creative combination of devolved responsibilities, long-term planning, intellectual excitement and high levels of personal involvement and responsibility for staff and students alike. This calls for the senior management of universities to be helped to a better understanding of the forms of management required to facilitate innovation, commitment and change.

Ninth, universities in particular should nurture within themselves and justify publicly a climate in which the unthinkable can be thought, in which research and scholarship of a completely non-utilitarian kind can be undertaken and where the search for knowledge can be celebrated as an end in itself. The justification is not simply that such conditions are fundamental to all basic research in science. It is that they are at the root of all creative endeavour in a vibrant culture and civilization and, in a fundamental way, the source of all thought about the values which ought to govern our lives.

Tenth, there is a contradiction to be resolved: Peter Scott (1995) has noted tellingly that mass higher education is positioned in the middle of one of the most acute dilemmas of postmodern society. To simplify: modern society depends on specialized bodies of knowledge to which only relatively few people have access. On the other hand, citizens and consumers need access to knowledge to make informed choices and to keep modernity – at least in its market-driven capitalistic forms – going.

Mass systems of higher education have opened the doors of educational opportunity to far more people than the older elite models. But they have done so in a world of cultural and moral fragmentation. Universities are therefore caught up in the cultural contradictions of modern societies. The critical rationality which is their Enlightenment inheritance is itself under question.

The link between knowledge and values, the idea that the search for knowledge was both a virtue in itself and one which helped people to understand the values that should govern their lives – one of the grand narratives of the post-Enlightenment modern world – has been broken by the development of an instrumental rationality related to scientific and technological requirements.

The challenge to higher education is thus twofold: to help the citizens of modern societies to know and understand more about the societies they live in and to be part of a wider public debate about the values which inform decisions in political and economic life.

The politics of dialogue

It is not enough, however, to argue for these goals and hope in some osmotic way that public opinion will exert itself through the ballot box. Nor can it be assumed that the ideas set out above are widely shared in the 'academic community'. They are not and it would be surprising if they were. Academics may complain about what is happening to them, but they remain among the prime beneficiaries of the system that employs them and many strongly support its present forms. It is necessary to engage key players in dialogue and to do so in ways which promise real change and a greater understanding of the options in higher education policy.

For each of the key players in higher education policy, the analysis set out in this chapter contains important messages, each of which should be seriously evaluated. Sir Ron Dearing's review of higher education is timely. We very much hope that those who contribute to it will not lose sight of the wider social purpose of higher education. To facilitate the Dearing debate, we urge the following points.

For government:

- Base fund higher education with resources adequate to the roles it must play.
- Steer higher education to a much stronger public service role.
- Support part-time students on an equal basis with full-time students.
- Require the development of a national system of credit accumulation and transfer flexible enough to incorporate the accreditation of prior learning and of work-based learning.
- Provide tax incentives to both employers and individuals to encourage a higher level of investment in training and lifelong learning.
- Require universities to clarify the precise ways in which they intend to play a stronger regional role and cooperate more effectively with other higher education institutions in their regions.
- Lift the strangulating bureaucratic pressure on universities and explore much more cost-effective and credible systems of quality audit, research evaluation, accountability and control.
- Reform the Higher Education Funding Councils to reinstate a buffer institution between the government and the universities which reflects a wider range of stakeholders and much greater democratic accountability.
- Develop a planning framework for higher education which devolves decisions and responsibilities to regional structures capable of responding to local needs for education and training, and which will require much higher levels of cooperation among institutions than currently exists.
- Have the courage to implement a system in which graduates pay a higher proportion of the costs of their tuition linked to their capacity to pay and in recognition of their greater lifelong earning.

For the universities themselves:

- Defend critical, basic research and scholarship as both the lifeblood of the intellect and the hallmark of a civilized society.
- Articulate, promote and defend their commitment to democratic values and their responsibility to be engaged directly in major public debates covering all matters of concern in modern society and to bring to these debates their resources of critical scholarship and research.
- Innovate outwards through active, committed engagement with the needs of the localities and regions they serve.
- Generate more income to reduce dependency on state funding. This is not a question of fund-raising; it is much more one of searching, in partnership with employers (public, private and the professions, national and international) for new work and long-term opportunities – in research, education and training – of an income-generating, mutually beneficial kind.

- Open up the curriculum to enable more flexible forms of study exploiting new information technologies and placing much greater emphasis on helping students to acquire a knowledge of how to learn.
- Develop the role of the university lecturer, together with change in current systems of reward and recognition, to enable staff to achieve the new institutional mission.
- Strive within their own systems of management to achieve much higher levels of staff and student involvement in decision-making and planning, balanced with much more effective structures of public accountability.
- Develop better mechanisms of strategic planning to anticipate change and define appropriate responses to it. Too much of higher education management is, like government policy itself, short-term and reactive.

For students:

- Expect high standards of teaching, learning, learning support and resources for effective study.
- Expect programmes of study to be relevant to personal and professional development needs and to include as a matter of course added value options in employment experience, information technology and foreign languages.
- Expect lifelong, flexible learning opportunities.
- Expect to pay some proportion of tuition costs as an affordable contribution to maintaining a system which should guarantee lifelong benefits.
- Expect a voice in the development of courses and the management of institutions; learn to use institutions of higher education rather than be processed by them.
- Expect to be held accountable for personal achievements and to make a positive contribution to the intellectual and cultural life of the institution and the communities it serves.

For employers and the professions:

- Seek to develop coherent, practical and long-term working links with higher education.
- Engage with higher education in partnerships to develop mutually beneficial research, training and strategic planning to contribute to economic development and employment growth.
- Develop frameworks for the accreditation and promotion of more effective systems of work-based, lifelong learning.
- Acknowledge an important role in helping higher education to contribute to the growth in sustainable employment opportunities. This public commitment must be matched by a private obligation to generate investment-led employment opportunities and further training for well qualified staff.

For the general public:

- Understand that higher education is part of society and vital to the development and promotion of the cultural and moral values upon which modern society and the quality of people's lives within it ultimately depends. Policies for the universities cannot be detached from discussions about how this society should develop and change. There has to be a critical space in the public spheres of modern society where intellectual honesty and ceaseless vigilance about social, economic and political developments has to be maintained, free of the patronage of governments and of other rich and powerful interest groups. Universities have a role to play, alongside an independent press and in the context of a lively democratic debate. They are not and never should be arbiters of morality; but they do have a part to play in sharpening up the moral discourses of modernity.

• Examine and judge how far universities meet the requirement to help build an educated public capable of evaluating critically the policies of governments or of making sense of the profound social and technical changes transforming the modern world. We have argued (in Chapter 1) that universities have a vital role in helping to build a society which is both socially just and economically efficient. How far they achieve this is something to be actively debated.

• Appreciate that universities are a rich resource, a treasure of new, creative and challenging ideas, learning, scholarship and research which meet the needs of some groups very well and touch hardly at all the needs of others. The question 'Who benefits?' is one which needs to be answered and kept under constant review.

• Debate the roles higher education could play – through teaching, scholarship and research – in helping to secure the social, economic and cultural regeneration of modern society.

Conclusions

We have deliberately avoided in this chapter the temptation to spell out a five-point plan of action or to specify any practical details of policy in higher education. This is not because it would not have been possible to do so; it is because there is a much more fundamental question about the ends of higher education to be settled before detailed work is done on how to provide the means to achieve them. The purposes of higher education cannot be separated from debate about the kind of society it is part of and is expected to contribute to. Too much of the debate about higher education in the past two decades has been narrowly focused on issues of resources and management. As the millennium approaches, it is time to lift the sights and transform our vision of what the future could be like.

The twentieth century was an age of extremes; the twenty-first will be no less challenging or threatening. There may well have been a loss of faith among intellectuals in the capacity of people in modern societies to plan, to anticipate the future, to debate options and to arrive at rational solutions to complex problems. The need for such thinking has not, however, diminished. Nor has our capacity to do it.

The old bargain between the university and society has, as David Robertson has argued in this volume, broken down. It has to be replaced with a new one that taxpayers, students and employers are prepared to support. The thrust of the analysis developed here is that the new bargain needs extensive, open debate and that universities themselves should inform that debate and be much more prepared than they have so far been to articulate their own missions alongside wider public goals. They themselves must change if they are to expect greater support from government and from within the society which ultimately funds them.

The evidence is that they will not change by themselves, that their own structures of management and leadership have rendered them incapable of radical change in the face of relentless pressure from government. If they are to 'learn their way out' of their current problems and not delude themselves through the kind of initiative fatigue and reactive change which has characterized them in the past decade, then they must develop stronger connections with broader constituencies of interest in society and take more seriously their obligations to inform public debates about the social purposes of higher education.

The report currently being prepared by Sir Ron Dearing on the future of higher education will make some headlines for a while; it may even bring about some welcome changes in current policies. Inevitably, however, its recommendations will be attempts to solve some of the problems of the past and to shore up a system badly creaking under the strain of its own contradictions. Beyond Dearing a more fundamental task will still remain: that of articulating and defending a vision of higher education which promotes world-class teaching and research and the democratic values without which such achievements are meaningless. If there is one lesson to be learned from the 'age of extremes' this is surely it: without a just, democratic, sustainable and productive society, a higher education worth the name has no future.

References

Barnett, R. (1993) *The Idea of Higher Education.* Buckingham, Open University Press/ SRHE.

Beare, H. and Slaughter, R. (1993) *Education for the Twenty-first Century.* London, Routledge.

Elliott, J. *et al.* (1996) *Communities and Their Universities: the Challenge of Lifelong Learning.* London, Lawrence and Wishart.

Fukuyama, F. (1993) *The End of History and the Last Man.* Harmondsworth, Penguin.

Galbraith, J. K. (1992) *The Culture of Contentment.* Harmondsworth, Penguin.

Gibbons, M. *et al.* (1994) *The New Production of Knowledge: the Dynamics of Science and Research in Contemporary Societies.* London, Sage.

Halsey, A. H. (1992) *The Decline of Donnish Dominion.* Oxford, Clarendon Press.

Havel, V. (1987) *Living within Truth*. London, Faber and Faber.

Keep, E. and Mayhew, K. (1995) The economic demand for higher education, and investing in people – two aspects of sustainable development in British higher education, in F. Coffield (ed.) *Higher Education in a Learning Society*. Durham, Durham University School of Education.

Kogan, M. and Kogan, D. (1983) *The Attack on Higher Education*. London, Kogan Page.

Mohan, J. (1996) Re-connecting the academy? Community involvement in American and British universities, in J. Elliott *et al.* (eds) *Communities and Their Universities: the Challenge of Lifelong Learning*. London, Lawrence and Wishart.

Scott, P. (1995) *The Meanings of Mass Higher Education*. Buckingham, Open University Press/SRHE.

Tawney, R. H. (1981) A national college of all souls, in *The Attack and Other Papers*. London, Spokesman.

Index

The Society for Research into Higher Education

The Society for Research into Higher Education exists to stimulate and coordinate research into all aspects of higher education. It aims to improve the quality of higher education through the encouragement of debate and publication on issues of policy, on the organization and management of higher education institutions, and on the curriculum and teaching methods.

The Society's income is derived from subscriptions, sales of its books and journals, conference fees and grants. It receives no subsidies, and is wholly independent. Its individual members include teachers, researchers, managers and students. Its corporate members are institutions of higher education, research institutes, professional, industrial and governmental bodies. Members are not only from the UK, but from elsewhere in Europe, from America, Canada and Australasia, and it regards its international work as among its most important activities.

Under the imprint *SRHE & Open University Press*, the Society is a specialist publisher of research, having some 60 titles in print. The Editorial Board of the Society's Imprint seeks authoritative research or study in the above fields. It offers competitive royalties, a highly recognizable format in both hardback and paperback and the worldwide reputation of the Open University Press.

The Society also publishes *Studies in Higher Education* (three times a year), which is mainly concerned with academic issues, *Higher Education Quarterly* (formerly *Universities Quarterly*), mainly concerned with policy issues, *Research into Higher Education Abstracts* (three times a year), and *SRHE News* (four times a year).

The Society holds a major annual conference in December, jointly with an institution of higher education. In 1994 the topic was 'The Student Experience' at the University of York. In 1995 it was 'The Changing University' at Heriot-Watt University in Edinburgh and in 1996, 'Working in Higher Education' at Cardiff Institute of Higher Education. Conferences in 1997 include 'Beyond the First Degree' at the University of Warwick.

The Society's committees, study groups and branches are run by the members. The groups at present include:

Teacher Education Study Group
Continuing Education Group
Staff Development Group
Excellence in Teaching and Learning

Benefits to members

Individual

Individual members receive:

- *SRHE News*, the Society's publications list, conference details and other material included in mailings.
- Greatly reduced rates for *Studies in Higher Education* and *Higher Education Quarterly*.
- A 35 per cent discount on all SRHE & Open University Press publications.
- Free copies of the Proceedings – commissioned papers on the theme of the Annual Conference.
- Free copies of *Research into Higher Education Abstracts*.
- Reduced rates for conferences.
- Extensive contacts and scope for facilitating initiatives.
- Reduced reciprocal memberships.
- Free copies of the *Register of Members' Research Interests*.

Corporate

Corporate members receive:

- All benefits of individual members, plus.
- Free copies of *Studies in Higher Education*.
- Unlimited copies of the Society's publications at reduced rates.
- Special rates for its members e.g. to the Annual Conference.
- The right to submit application for the Society's research grants.

Membership details: SRHE, 3 Devonshire Street, London W1N 2BA, UK. Tel: 0171 637 2766. Fax: 0171 637 2781. email: srhe@clus1.ulcc.ac.uk
Catalogue: SRHE & Open University Press, Celtic Court, 22 Ballmoor, Buckingham MK18 1XW. Tel: 01280 823388. Fax: 01280 823233. email: enquiries@openup.co.uk

THE MEANINGS OF MASS HIGHER EDUCATION

Peter Scott

This book is the first systematic attempt to analyse the growth of mass higher education in a specifically British context, while seeking to develop more theoretical perspectives on this transformation of elite university systems into open post-secondary
education systems. It is divided into three main sections. The first examines the
evolution of British higher education and the development of universities and other
institutions. The second explores the political, social and economic context within
which mass systems are developing. What are the links between post-industrial society, a post-Fordist economy and the mass university? The third section discusses
the links between massification and wider currents in intellectual and scientific
culture.

Contents
*Preface – Introduction – Structure and institutions – State and society – Science and culture
– Understanding mass higher education – Notes – Index.*

208pp   0 335 19442 7 (Paperback)   0 335 19443 5 (Hardback)

THE LIMITS OF COMPETENCE
KNOWLEDGE, HIGHER EDUCATION AND SOCIETY

Ronald Barnett

Competence is a term which is making its entrance in the university. How might it be understood at this level? *The Limits of Competence* takes an uncompromising line, providing a sustained critique of the notion of competence as wholly inadequate for higher education.

Currently, we are seeing the displacement of one limited version of competence by another even more limited interpretation. In the older definition – one of academic competence – notions of disciplines, objectivity and truth have been central. In the new version, competence is given an operational twist and is marked out by know-how, competence and skills. In this operationalism, the key question is not 'What do students understand?' but 'What can students do?'

The book develops an alternative view, suggesting that, for our universities, a third and heretical conception of human being is worth considering. Our curricula might, instead, offer an education for life.

Contents
Introduction – Part 1: Knowledge, higher education and society: The learning society? – A certain way of knowing? – We are all clerks now – Part 2: The new vocabulary: 'Skills' and 'vocationalism' – 'Competence' and 'outcomes' – 'Capability' and 'enterprise' – Part 3: The lost vocabulary: Understanding – Critique – Interdisciplinarity – Wisdom – Part 4: Competence reconsidered: Two rival versions of competence – Beyond competence – Retrospect and coda – Bibliography – Index.

222pp   0 335 19341 2 (Paperback)   0 335 19070 7 (Hardback)

LEADING ACADEMICS
Robin Middlehurst

At a time of major change in higher education, the quality of university leadership is an issue of key importance. Whether heading a research team, planning curriculum innovations, managing a department or running an institution, effective leadership is required. Yet how well is the idea of leadership understood? How is leadership practised in the academic world? What special characteristics are needed to lead autonomous professionals?

This book, based on research in universities, is the first comprehensive examination of leadership in British higher education. Robin Middlehurst critiques contemporary ideas of leadership and examines their relevance to academe. She explores the relationship between models of leadership and practice at different levels of the institution. She argues for a better balance between leadership and management in universities in order to increase the responsiveness and creativity of higher education.

Contents
Part 1: Thinking about leadership – What is leadership? – The new leadership – Organizational images – Leadership and academe: traditions and change – Part 2: Practising leadership – Institutional leaders – Collective leadership – Leading departments – Individuals and leadership – Part 3: Developing leadership – Leadership learning – Endings and beginnings – Bibliography – Index.

c.192pp   0 335 09988 2 (Paperback)   0 335 09989 0 (Hardback)

THE LEARNING UNIVERSITY
TOWARDS A NEW PARADIGM?

Chris Duke

Chris Duke addresses issues central to the evolution and future of higher education. He examines assumptions by and about universities, their changing environments, the new terminologies and their adaptation to new circumstances. He explores how far universities *are* learning, changing and adapting; and whether they are becoming different kinds of institutions or whether only the rhetoric is altering. He is particularly concerned with how far universities, as key teaching and learning organizations, are adopting the new paradigm of lifelong learning. He discusses how far the concepts and requirements for institution-wide continuing education have been identified and internalized in institutional planning; are they, for instance, reflected in programmes of staff development (in the continuing education of staff in higher education)? *Is* a new paradigm of university education and organization really emerging?

Contents
Old assumptions and new practices – Change and higher education: the new discourse – Mission, aims and objectives – What may be new? – Out of the box: continuing education university-wide – Finishing school or service station: what mix? – Access, quality and success: old and new criteria – Staff development and organizational learning – The fallacy of the ivory tower – Appendix – Bibliography – Index.

160pp   0 335 15653 3 (Paperback)